Other Books by Daniel Berrigan

CONSEQUENCES: TRUTH & 1967

DARK NIGHT OF RESISTANCE

ENCOUNTERS: POETRY

FALSE GODS, REAL MEN

LOVE, LOVE AT THE END

NIGHT FLIGHT TO HANOI

NO BARS TO MANHOOD

NO ONE WALKS WATERS

THEY CALL US DEAD MEN

TRIAL OF THE CATONSVILLE NINE

WORLD FOR WEDDING RING

"AMERICA IS HARD TO FIND"

GEOGRAPHY OF FAITH
(with Robert Coles)

TRIAL POEMS
(with Thomas Lewis)

ABSURD CONVICTIONS, MODEST HOPES

Daniel Berrigan

ABSURD CONVICTIONS, MODEST HOPES

Conversations after Prison
with Lee Lockwood

Random House   New York

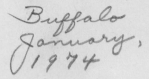

Buffalo
January,
1974

Library of Congress Cataloging in Publication Data

LOCKWOOD, LEE.
DANIEL BERRIGAN: ABSURD CONVICTIONS, MODEST HOPES.

1. BERRIGAN, DANIEL.   2. PRISONS—CONNECTICUT—DANBURY.
I. BERRIGAN, DANIEL.   II. TITLE.
III. TITLE: ABSURD CONVICTIONS, MODEST HOPES.
BX4705.B3845L6   322.4'4'0924 [B]   72–2700
ISBN 0–394–48228–X

Manufactured in the United States of America
by Kingsport Press, Inc., Kingsport, Tenn.

2 4 6 8 9 7 5 3

First Edition

We dedicate this book to all resisters
in American prisons—Prisoners of War
in their own country.

—D.B. & L.L.

Introductory Note

The Federal Correctional Institution at Danbury, Connecticut, is as anonymous as the lives of the prisoners therein incarcerated. It is not to be found on any road maps; no road signs direct the way. Driving in from New York or Boston—as I did many times during the seventeen months that it was the temporary home of Daniel Berrigan—you leave Interstate 84, a busy superhighway, and turn northward on Route 37, away from the city of Danbury. Route 37 is an unimproved country road. After a quick taste of suburbia—a shopping center, a modern movie theater, three or four plastic gas stations—you quickly lose the feeling of civilization as the road begins to wind and climb. Twenty-five miles to the north, high in the Connecticut hills, are the fashionable, converted farmhouses of the exurban arts establishment of New York: Arthur Miller, William Styron, Leonard Bernstein, et al., who dwell in pastoral comfort amid tall oaks and the ruins of stone walls. But here, in the foothills, the trees are third-growth and the landscape is distinctly middle-American: scattered clusters of Victorian clapboard houses in need of repair and paint, an occasional roadside tavern, a body shop, huckstering billboards rising through the hillside brush.

Ascending through this blighted landscape, the road, barely wide enough to contain two lanes of traffic, continues to wind treacherously around its northering axis as it climbs, following the eastern ridge of an ancient river. The soil is rocky and the foliage rural now; you are in the country. A sudden flock of stores and modest homes marks the village of Pembroke, gone almost before you have noticed it in yet another swing of the road. Climbing and curving still, you pass the Pembroke Day Nursery on the right and the Hallas Farm Market on the left. Then, without warning, on the right-hand side a break in the trees reveals an enormous vista of closely cut, grassy slopes receding upward toward the horizon and, in the far distance, the insipid, low profile of the penitentiary. In winter, when I saw it for the first time, the hillside was buried under a glossy skin of frozen snow, and the prison, a buff-colored structure of cement hugging the distant crest, seemed, thus surrounded by gleaming whiteness that proffered no sign of life, as extragalactic as a DEW-Line installation in the Arctic wastes of Canada. In such a landscape, I thought, who could live in hope?

Later, I learned that although the penitentiary "owns" more than a hundred acres of the land around it, prisoners are never allowed to set foot upon any of it.

The only taste of the rehabilitative juices of nature permitted them is the few hundred yards of level turf within the prison quadrangle, at certain brief moments of the day and on weekends. As for the vast property outside the penitentiary walls, it is DMZ territory: defoliated, unlived in, a buffer zone between prison life and "the real world."

The Danbury penitentiary is a "medium security institution." I am no expert on federal prisons, but I have come to know that this means something between guarded fortresses like Sing Sing and Alcatraz, and minimum security installations such as the work farm at Allenwood, Pennsylvania. At Danbury, there are no barbed-wire fences, no armed guards manning the watchtowers. Driving toward it on Route 37, you miss the entrance if you are not careful; it is marked only by a small bronze plaque affixed to a low stone pillar, the plaque inscribed "Federal Correctional Institution" and engraved not with a hammer-and-sickle or a skull-and-crossbones but with a crossed lock-and-key. Turning here, you ascend the smooth blacktop approach road, unchallenged and unwatched, with nothing but rolling fields visible on all sides. It is always a jolt to reach the top and see, at once, the penitentiary and its three large parking lots jammed with the cars of prison workers and visitors, an evidence of teeming life totally unexpected and totally at odds with the impersonality of the surroundings.

It was in this unholy place that I first came to visit Father Daniel Berrigan, Jesuit priest, poet and convicted felon, in December 1970, four months after his capture on Block Island. I had met Dan Berrigan while he was "underground," to use his term, in May of that year, when we had begun collaborating on a documentary film about his experiences as a "fugitive from injustice."

) XI (

My last sight of him had been in early August in a church in Germantown, Pennsylvania, where he made a surprise appearance, delivering an impassioned sermon on the need for Americans of conscience to resist the war in Vietnam, even at the risk of the security of their own lives. Then he had dropped from sight. Nine days later, he was in the hands of the FBI.

For most men of intelligence and sensitivity who find themselves in jail—and there are thousands of them in prisons all across the country—a prison sentence is a sentence out of the real world into limbo, a time when one's outside involvements fail or drop away, a time spent in hibernation from the world, in just getting by. As Father Berrigan describes so movingly in this book, every aspect of prison life leads in this direction; not toward rehabilitation, the mythic goal that prisons are supposed to serve, but toward dehumanization, toward idleness, toward the transformation of the inmate into a compliant vegetable.

Fortunately, this did not happen to Dan Berrigan. For all that he suffered during his seventeen months at Danbury—and it was considerable—he was never idle or compliant. He made his presence felt, both inside and outside the walls, and on some, perhaps a handful, left a profound and permanent mark. (I dare say that the warden and the Catholic chaplain will never forget him either.)

It was Dan Berrigan's miraculous luck that it suited the purposes of the federal government to transfer his brother Philip to Danbury within a few weeks of Dan's arrival—good luck for Philip too, it should be added. Why the Justice Department should have brought the two brothers together, where they were bound to be a much greater problem for prison authorities than apart, is still a mystery. It possibly had to do with the FBI's belief, then still unknown to the public, that the Berrigans were plotting a citizen's arrest of Henry Kissinger; having both of them under one roof should make it easier to keep tabs on their visitors and to gather further evidence. But, whatever the reason, it was the first time that Dan and Phil had been together for any protracted period of time since childhood—and they made the most of it.

For one thing, they found a ready ministry at Danbury. Though they were not permitted to conduct services or to preach—Federal Bureau of Prisons regulations stipulate that inmates may not practice their professions—they did serve mass on Sunday. Also, twice a week in the evenings, each of them met with a separate small group of Catholics to study the gospels. In addition, the two brothers were able to initiate a sort of "great books" discussion class on contemporary themes, which at times included as many as thirty inmates. As Dan Berrigan relates, this was by far the most fruitful activity of their prison experiences, and I have spoken to former inmates since released from Danbury who told me that being in that group was one of the most important experiences in their lives. Amidst the dull fabric of triviality and irrelevancy that is prison, it provided virtually their only opportunity to relate to the pressing political and social issues of our time and to examine what their own responsibilities as adults in the outside world might be when they returned to it.

On a more practical level, the questions of conscience raised and discussed in that class led directly to the work-and-hunger strike at Danbury in July 1971, in which several dozen inmates participated (at which time Philip Berrigan and ten others were shipped temporarily to the Medical Facility at Springfield, Missouri, until they ended their fast), and to the general work strike against the war in January 1972, in which virtually the entire prison population took part. In both cases, the core organizers were members of the Berrigans' discussion group.

On November 27, 1970, FBI Director J. Edgar Hoover made public his now-famous charge that Daniel and Philip Berrigan were the ringleaders of "an incipient plot" to kidnap a high government official and destroy heating tunnels in Washington, D.C. When I visited them a few weeks later, I found Dan and Phil in a frolicsome mood; they felt Hoover had gone too far and that the charges would never be substantiated. However, on January 27, 1971, an indictment was issued in Harrisburg, Pennsylvania, formally charging Philip Berrigan and five others (four of them members of the so-called "Catholic Left") with the conspiracy, and naming Dan Berrigan as an "unindicted co-conspirator." However far removed from reality this seemed, the indictment was serious business, and not long afterward the Berrigans began holding weekly meetings with the other defendants and lawyers at the Danbury jail to plan their defense.

The gravity (and the perplexity) of the situation was intensified on May 2, when a new, "superceding" indictment was issued. It named two new defendants and included the additional charge that all eight had conspired to raid draft boards and obstruct the Selective Service System. Throughout the long year between the first indictment and the commencement of the trial, these conferences with lawyers and defendants would occupy a major part of the time and energy of both Berrigans.

(Though Daniel's name was inexplicably dropped altogether from the second indictment, he was permitted to continue taking part in the meetings because the first indictment was still, technically, in effect.)

Those indicted were: Father Philip Berrigan SSJ; Sister Elizabeth McAlister RSHM (a Catholic nun); Fathers Joseph Wenderoth and Neil McLaughlin (parish priests from Baltimore); Anthony and Mary Scoblick (an ex-priest and ex-nun whose wedding in 1970 had been attended by dozens of FBI agents searching for the fugitive Daniel Berrigan); Dr. Eqbal Ahmad (a Pakistani scholar and Fellow of the Adlai Stevenson Institute in Chicago); and J. Theodore Glick (a young antiwar activist). All those indicted except Ahmad had been involved in antiwar draft board actions. Dr. Ahmad is a close friend of Daniel Berrigan and had helped organize his underground activities.

Prison life took a serious toll on Dan Berrigan physically, a toll which at times affected his spirits. Never blessed with robust health to begin with, he had entered prison suffering from a "herniated esophagus," a condition somewhat like an ulcer, which required, for cure or control, a bland and greaseless diet and extra quantities of milk that he could not obtain at Danbury. Often, during a visit, he would disappear momentarily from the visiting room for a slug of Maalox to quiet his troubled chest. He also had an arthritic elbow that required periodic shots of cortisone directly into the bone, a treatment he found far more painful than the disease. Toward the end of his stay, he developed a painfulness in his lower back that was later diagnosed as a form of arthritis of the spine. While not dangerous, it was (and is) seriously discomforting, especially at night, when it forces him to sleep on a board or, more often, as he did in hotels where we stayed together after his release, on the floor.

More dangerous was the attack that almost killed him in June 1971. While preparing him for dental work, the assistant administering the Novocaine accidentally pierced an artery; the instantaneous result was a "massive allergic shock" to his respiratory system, which rendered Dan unconscious and momentarily halted his breathing. The prison authorities, understandably, were scared to death. As soon as they could get his lungs going again with adrenalin and oxygen, they shipped him off to the Danbury Hospital. He remained there in the intensive-care unit for several days until doctors were certain that he had not suffered a heart attack. Dan's funny-sad account of this escapade, of hanging near death with death all around him, of the strange people who came to visit him and the personages he encountered in the hospital, will be found within these pages.

Philip, by contrast, was always in boisterous good health and spirits, even when the world around him looked blackest. Graced with a large, muscular physique which he kept from flabbiness with daily mile-runs around the quadrangle and a regime of push-ups and other strenuous calisthenics, he always seemed the strongest and handsomest man in the visiting room, and he was obviously looked up to by the other inmates. I recall visiting him once just after his return from Springfield, Missouri. He had lost twenty pounds during his fast, but he had gained it all back and looked as fit as ever. His presence at Danbury probably kept his brother's state of health from deteriorating even further, for he made Dan watch his diet carefully, exercise regularly, and take naps when he felt tired—in short, he forced

Dan to exercise a kind of self-concern that simply would not have occurred to him had he been on his own.

In August 1971, having served the necessary minimums of their respective sentences, Daniel and Philip Berrigan were granted hearings by the parole board. Parole was summarily denied; as is customary, no explanation was given for the decision. The following January, the Federal Parole Board in Washington, D.C., agreed to hear an appeal in the case of Dan Berrigan, on the ground that there was "new evidence" on the condition of his health. To everyone's surprise, including that of his lawyers, parole was now granted, and Dan was scheduled for release on February 24, 1972.

"There are just some things, I hesitate to count them, I don't do very well," Dan Berrigan once wrote to me from Danbury. "One of them, it develops, is long term jail. We shd. have gotten a habeas something or other and put me to work in someone's corn patch where I could have been really green thumbed & creative. Alas?"

Restriction on his creativity was one of the deepest deprivations imposed on him by prison regulations. To offset it, and to brighten up his letters to friends, Dan took to inscribing short poems within his correspondence, often embellishing them with imaginative designs carved out of rubber erasers and stamped in watercolors. Here are a few of them, with the dates on which they were sent:

(APRIL 17, 1971)

teach my eyes to rejoice in one shivering
budless tree
aster

) XVII (

framed in a barred window
wide existence
narrowed to a keeper's eye

(MAY 8, 1971)

The tulips are jailyard blooms, they wear
        bravery with a difference.
    They are born here, die here
making them, by excess of suffering
            and transfiguration
                of suffering, ours.

(SEPT. 27, 1971)

The ideogram
is of a man
standing by
his word.
fidelity. free-
dom consequent
on the accepted
necessity of
standing where
one's
word leads.
wherever.
Hebrew prophets &
psalmist also
struck the theme
bodies belong
where words
are
though the com-

) XVIII (

mon run of exper-
ience be
that the flesh
shrinks as
the word
inflates.
the synthesis
would seem
to be: no
matter. (or
better) never
the less.

(OCT. 23, 1971)

the eye regards the
heart. a western view
the heart regards
the eye. as the Chinese
say
and the great world
between
    known both by
caliper and transfus-
ion
    rigor and gift.
I had rather, if I
must, choose among
methods.
    but I cannot

On February 24, 1972, at eight-thirty in the snowy
morning, Dan was released from the Danbury penitentiary to the cheering of hundreds of relatives, friends

) **XIX** (

and supporters who had waited warmly in the cold. The conversations which appear in this book are the result of tape recordings which we commenced in New York City three days later; they were terminated early in April, before the end of the trial in Harrisburg (which he was able to visit on two occasions) and the sentencing of his brother. The transcripts were then edited and reorganized by both of us, working closely together, into this final manuscript. For me at least—and I hope for Dan— it was a stimulating and rewarding time.

Lee Lockwood

Boston, May 1972

ABSURD CONVICTIONS, MODEST HOPES

1

LEE LOCKWOOD: You've been out of jail three days now. How does it feel to be free?

DANIEL BERRIGAN: It's like an electric circus. But I'm coping better than I thought I would. I thought there would be a lot of reentry shock, but I haven't felt it. What has struck me is that there are so many hungry people around, to whom my being out means a great deal more than I would have ever predicted or felt.

LL: How so?

DB: I had really no impression that it would be such an event for people. And the inconvenience they went through, the long wait in the snow there, outside the prison, and then the long wait for the liturgy; well, that was overwhelming. I think people have been going through a starvation diet in heroism; otherwise I couldn't explain it. Not that I qualify. But they think I do, and that's sobering indeed.

LL: Is it too big a responsibility?

DB: Well, I just don't feel responsible in that sense of being poured into their mold. But I certainly feel that I ought to ponder this all very deeply, in the light of whatever is coming.

LL: Have there been any other surprises about life in the outside world compared to life in jail?

DB: The New York taxis are a great surprise! It's almost like being locked into a marshal's car again, with all that hardware around and those incredible barriers against human beings touching or meeting one another. That came down on me in a terrible way, a sign of the fear and hostility that reign in public, where cabbies think that they have to protect their lives that way. I'm sure that they have good reason for doing it, but I find it horrible.

LL: You've always liked New York a lot.

DB: Very much.

LL: Do you still like it as much as ever?

DB: Oh, yes.

LL: What have you been doing?

DB: Well, just about everything, I guess. We went to a play yesterday—*Two Gentlemen of Verona*—and we had all sorts of gatherings in the course of the day. And today I was on *Meet the Press.* I walked the streets very quietly for about an hour this morning with Jerry and Carol and Philip, their son. We went all through Chinatown the other day and Little Italy. The city is very exciting in its variety of human beings. That's the real beauty of it. You know, I like being around here again!

LL: Do you miss Danbury?

) 4 (

DB: I miss the people when I have a moment to think of them. And when I do, it's a very familiar ache, because I know what they go through and what the daily squirrel round is like. I can visualize them at any point of the day and what they're doing, because it's the same every day. Except for the very small number who have some reason for doing it, it's a horrible flattening-out of lives into tin cans, into waste, and that's very difficult to think of. I can justify this for myself, and for the resisters, and for the other prisoners we were able to touch and awaken. But the vast majority are just up there walking circles night and day.

LL: So the reality of Danbury hasn't been replaced by the reality of the outside world in your consciousness yet?

DB: I'm really not in Danbury emotionally. I'm there when I think about the people there. As far as any scars or that kind of nonsense, I don't have any. But I guess, in a sense, I am between two worlds right now.

LL: Is that feeling a little upsetting?

DB: No, not exactly. It's really a kind of high.

LL: So far, what's the greatest pleasure of being out of jail?

DB: It comes down to something very simple but very precious: it's the presence of friends again. I just breathe better. I don't have this dragging of isolation with my energies tied up. It's very hard to express, but I no longer have a sense of imminent death or dismemberment, of feeling like a moral basket-case. In prison I felt sandpapered in the spirit, in the sense that it was very hard to come on affectionately and spontaneously with people; you feel so much of the best part of yourself kind of withering, you know? Now all of me is awakening again. I feel coming alive!

) 5 (

LL: I don't think you've ever described what happened the day you were arrested on Block Island. When were you first aware that the jig was up?

DB: Well, the weather that morning was very bad. There was a huge nor'easter blowing. I had gotten up late and was walking outside the house, and Bill Stringfellow noticed from the kitchen that there were these fellows prowling around the bushes. So we got our binoculars on them and immediately became suspicious, because *they* also had binoculars. Then, as far as I can recall, Bill went out there and talked to them, and they said they were "bird watchers." And he said, "It's a funny day for your trade! Furthermore, you are trespassing." At that point, I think, they told him who they were, and the cars came roaring up.

LL: You were in the house by that time?

DB: Bill and Tony had called me into the house when things got tricky. So I was sitting in the living room when suddenly these two cars roared in, and I knew it was all up. In fact, I think I was the first of the three of us to realize that. So I just went outside.

LL: How did you feel at that moment?

DB: Well, I was momentarily stunned. And then, you know, I just said, "Well, here we are—next chapter!"

They frisked me and put me into the car, and I remember thinking at the time, as I sat there and contemplated the ruins of my kingdom, that St. Ignatius had said that it would take him fifteen minutes to adjust himself if the Jesuits were suddenly erased from the face of the earth. So I figured that if he could do that in fifteen, I should do this in five. (Laughing)

So, on the way to the Coast Guard station, with the agents chortling away in the car and getting off all these incredible pieties, I just gathered my spirits and said, "Forget it." Also, there was a great deal of pride to it, a sort of machismo—I wasn't about to show them that there was any real victory involved in taking me.

Then, on the boat trip back to the mainland, I made up my mind that the press would probably be waiting when I got there. And I thought to myself, "Well, how should I appear?" And I decided that the best thing I could do for my friends was to smile.

LL: Were you able to talk to the FBI agents who arrested you?

DB: Oh, yes. They were very anxious to get reactions from me. I think it was their way of getting a bit of revenge in, showing that they were good Catholics and that they were doing this as Catholics, that "the priest" was theirs at last. One of them, in fact, told me that he was a Jesuit "grad," and that he took particular satisfaction in serving "the greater glory of God." Since that was the Jesuit motto, he felt very good about it; this project, this capture, was "to the greater glory of God." He told me, "I said to myself when I took you: 'A.M.D.G.!'"*

LL: Looking back after eighteen months in jail, are you still pleased with your experience in the "underground"?

DB: Oh, yes. That was one of the richest and happiest times of my life. I couldn't imagine how it could have gone better or how we could have accomplished more in that short time.

LL: What do you think you accomplished?

DB: Well, it's not too easy to formulate. I think of my writing and moving among people, and a lot of very in-

* "A.M.D.G.," "Ad Majorem Dei Gloriam," is the official motto of the Jesuit Order.

tensive rapping with families. Then there was the idea
that one could, without violence, attach a lot of people
to a serious moral movement and could function in a
rather graceful and loose way, and survive, and have a
certain impact on the whole movement. I think at that
time it was one of the interesting things going on. It certainly was for me.

LL: I think there's no doubt about that. The question
could be asked, however, if it produced any lasting effect. While you were at large and popping up in the press
every other week, you were the center of interest for
many people. Since your capture, however, there doesn't
seem to have been anything happening around what you
were doing and saying.

DB: In a sense I think the objection is well taken. But
in another sense, what we're trying to deal with is the
long haul. There's no doubt about the fact that we're in
for a very long struggle. And there just need to be—
from time to time—some kinds of clues or signs which
will give hope and which people can remember and draw
on. I don't think one can always expect people to gather
immediately around a certain person as you suggest. My
case, take it or leave it, was unique. It was just a start.
As someone said to me after I was taken: "The best we
can say is that a seed was planted. And we don't know
what the flower is going to be."

I don't want to be mystical about it, but I think we're
just at the beginning of everything, so we really can't
be overly analytical. Almost any movement in the direction of creating some hope, of bringing people together,
I believe, is valuable. And that's what I think happened
to me.

Let me say this too. Last Christmas, in jail, I spent
hours upon hours upon hours going over a deluge of

Christmas mail. It came from the hundreds of people who wrote to me because of August 1970, because they saw a certain continuity, and because in a bad time they drew hope and sustenance from it, were "existing," they said, "a little bit more hopefully." I think all these things are hard to put down on paper, hard to tab up, but I think they are real, nonetheless.

LL: I suppose that the question I'm trying to ask is: What do all these people do besides writing to you? It seems to me that while you were at large there were many individuals who harbored you and helped you and were ready to engage in all sorts of activities supportive of your efforts. But when you were taken out of circulation these same individuals apparently had no way of focusing their energies or of giving implementation to their aspirations. If I'm right, don't you think it's possible that your underground experience may have been a waste of time? Or is it enough simply to plant "seeds" and hope that something worthwhile will emerge eventually?

DB: I really don't know against what yardstick you measure all of this, because everything we do is being done for the first time if it's valuable. And the whole movement is so youthful—not to say infantile—that we need, it seems to me, a wide variety of experimental things going on. Now, the fact that *nothing* is going on right now is, to me, no more than a fact. I don't know what conclusions to draw from it except that people are very tired, very frustrated; they're worn out from struggling against a power that seems absolutely untouchable and they need time to recoup and to recover themselves.

You can't keep up this level of energy indefinitely, organizing against a blank wall. So, I'm not seriously disturbed if people are in a momentary hiatus, gathering and thinking things over and looking into their heads and lives. I hope that's taking place. In other words, I hope that people haven't just *given up*. And I really don't know. But who does? Who does?

In prison, I read Isaac Deutscher's three-volume life of Trotsky. And I was encouraged and helped by the many analogies that I saw between what operated in czarist Russia and what operates here in America today. It seems to me that people of that time had to prepare for a lifelong haul, to face long, long plateaus of discouragement, the realization that those early movements broke up repeatedly before they were really formed. So many of those young people who went around Russia raising hell of one kind or another were destroyed, or picked up, imprisoned, exiled, were obliged to start over again—all this over a period of thirty, forty, or fifty years before any real fruition came. And I think it could be argued that the American Establishment is at least as persistent and powerful as the czarist was.

This is part of the maturing of the movement that Americans have never taken into account. Our thinking about social change is childish; it raises false hopes. We apply to human change the analogies and experiences that we have drawn from technology. We conclude that since we have done so much so quickly in mechanical fields and in pure science, we can do the same thing with one another. And that simply isn't the way that human beings are, I'm afraid—either here or in Vietnam or in Cuba or anywhere else. The spiritual dismantling of the American empire is going to consume at least our lifetime, and perhaps the lifetime of the next generation.

Understanding this, to be in prison or to be underground is what one makes of it. Every period of one's life can be valuable or useless in proportion as one brings resources to it and gathers people about it. Almost everything we try is remote from the outcome that we hope for; everything is equally remote from that outcome. Which is not to say that everything is equally valuable or useless, but that we don't know quite enough yet about what is crucial and what is not. In the meantime, we might just as well undergo what good people have always undergone, whether it's jail or underground or exile or anything else, and find out what happens there.

LL: You were "underground" nearly four months. During that period of time, you made several public appearances while managing to keep one step ahead of the massive FBI dragnet that was pursuing you. Those months, in fact, have become something of a legend in the annals of the antiwar movement. And yet, in spite of all that has been written about that period, it's very hard to get a full picture of what you were doing all that time.

DB: I think part of the difficulty is that the whole thing was so experimental and improvisational, and that I had so few models to go by except those out of rather remote history and of other cultures—that is to say, other Jesuits or other priests, other social crises that people like me have had to face. But maybe I could speak of some things in general; then we can talk about them more particularly.

I felt that I had two responsibilities. One of them was mainly a matter of spirit, a matter of my own growth and what I took to be my responsibility toward the Church. And the second was a matter of my public responsibility. Under the first rubric, I worked very hard at becoming what I would call "a contemplative," someone who had an interior, who was not merely a throwaway or part of a castaway culture but was connecting with his own history and tradition. That meant giving time to the world of the spirit, the world of my own spirit. So I would spend at least an hour and sometimes two or three hours a day meditating on the New Testament. That was my main source. Sometimes there was other reading that I thought offered a particular clue to where I was and where I was trying to go. I remember reading some of the underground poems of Pablo Neruda and spending a long time meditating on those, because I thought that they were in a sense a gloss on the New Testament text for me.

Well, very briefly, the second part was of course much more complex and dangerous and brought me continually into the public eye. I was trying to say to the public why I had avoided jail at that point, why I thought it was important to stay at large as long as I could, why I felt I owed no present obligation to American justice and would be taken by the law only under duress and at their initiative—that I would not surrender—and why I felt that the war issue was more grievous and more important than ever. I was trying to say all these things by appearing on television and by preaching in churches and by writing furiously for all kinds of publications; in general by being available in any ways that our imaginations could come up with.

LL: How did you decide to go underground in the first place?

DB: We had a meeting in Washington about a month before we were to surrender—that would take it back into March of '70. The Catonsville people were all present for that except for David Darst, who had died. We sat around in Washington for a day discussing the implications of our summons to prison and how we were going to respond to it. And out of that day, as well as I can remember, came the basic decisions of the four of us who were not going to appear: George Mische, Mary Moylan, my brother Philip and myself.

There had been a parallel feeling at Cornell, and I was certain of a supportive community for the enterprise, which was crucial. Gradually, the connection with the "America Is Hard to Find" weekend, which Cornell students and faculty were in the process of organizing, became apparent to us. We saw that it could be a really attractive event for the movement, an event in which I might appear and then disappear once more.

LL: Had you decided to disappear beforehand? A lot of people have said that it was a kind of spontaneous decision that you made only at the last minute.

DB: We had decided to live with the judge's summons when it came. Then we were going to play it by ear.

Up to the night I surfaced, our decision had been to appear and surrender. My intention was just to make a symbolic point—simply to show that I had a certain command over my life and freedom. But nothing long-term was planned at that time. Remember, I'd already been underground for almost two weeks. We felt that even two weeks would really get the word around the country and excite a lot of interest. Certain other alternatives were also in the air at the time, and there were discussions about them. But I thought they were very academic; since I believed the FBI would just pick me up that night whether I liked it or not. So whether or not to appear at Cornell seemed to be the main question. And when it was clear there would be huge numbers of people there, I said, "Sure, let's go, go with a bang!"

But the fact that the other possibility was on our

minds was evidenced by the speed with which we were able to execute another disappearance from Barton Hall, under the puppet.

LL: Was that spontaneous, the puppet act?

DB: Well, as I recall, it was only planned about half an hour in advance. Someone came to me and said, "Wouldn't you like to disappear again?" And I looked around and thought for a moment and said, "Sure—let's go." And they said, "Well, wait for the word from us," and then they did some dickering with the Bread and Puppet Theatre people. And the next word to me was, "The lights are going out very soon, because a rock band is appearing, and at that moment we'll go backstage and you just follow instructions." Which I did.

LL: And you came out on the other side of the looking-glass?

DB: Yes; wondrously and very excitingly, the whole thing worked. The next thing I remember very vividly is speeding through the dark in a panel truck with a deflated puppet in the back, now bereft of me, and about three or four of us chortling our way into the woods—having escaped very narrowly, because the FBI was hot on us. But we changed cars quickly, and it was easy from then on.

LL: I guess what I'm interested in knowing, if *you* know, is why you decided not to go to jail. It was a very sudden decision—what changed your mind?

DB: Our minds were never firm in one direction or the other. We were looking for what would happen that night. I would say I was resigned to going to jail that night, but I was also hopeful and open to alternatives that might occur, even though not much seemed possible.

LL: You mean, you went to the festival that night looking for a sign about what to do?

DB: Your way of putting it appeals to me because of the heavy Biblical influence of the night itself: in the middle of a "freedom Seder," when the prophet Elias has been invoked on behalf of all who are in trouble with the law, then I suddenly appear. To me the word "providential" is not too strong to explain the consequent happenings. I really believe there was a special providence over that night, that we were not invoking the Prophet of God in vain for protection, and that the response was beyond anyone's expectation, as the next months proved.

LL: Do you believe that Divine Providence works for you in a general way, that it hangs over your life?

DB: Well, I don't have any "general" notions about this, because I don't think that Providence is generalized. I think there's a very particular, personal providence over every living being, and that this providence is not a matter of my taking it or leaving it, if I'm a believer; that it's announced by Jesus in very definite terms in the most horrendous and difficult personal circumstances. Jesus declares that God's eye is on the sparrow, but then He has to believe it Himself, when He is before Pilate and Herod and on the Cross. These things have a way of becoming concrete in the sense that you either say "yes" to them or else you say "no" to them and go another way.

What I want to avoid here is the idea that Providence is connected with a special immunity from misfortune. That would be magic, a debased religion that Billy Graham might be interested in, or other charlatans like him, who would say, in effect, "Because I believe, I stand apart from the common fate; I can be spared the common suffering." I don't believe that at all. I don't believe it's true of Jesus. I think the connection between His life and mine is a passionate, loving belief such as would be true between brother and brother; and then a willingness, which is very difficult, to embrace the fate of mankind in His own flesh, in His own death—and the cutting off of many of His own hopes. Outside of that formulation, I think religion slides away from faith and takes on an expectation of magical results.

LL: You never felt there was a kind of magic, while you were underground, about your ability to move around almost at will and keep eluding the law?

DB: No. I don't think there was any magic to it at all. I think it was a time when we were cast in a very naked way—myself and all the people associated with me—we were cast upon Providence, upon God. Which is to say, very simply: upon one another. That situation I would give a particular name to: I would call it "providential," because my friends were there. Others would say: well, friends always gather when somebody is in need or when somebody has a good idea, especially a good idea which endangers him. These other interpretations don't put me off, but I have my own.

It was not magical in the sense that we were being plucked by the hair from the FBI at certain points of danger. The danger was always there, and the danger operated as it would operate if there were no God, if one can indulge in that kind of hypothesis. But the difference was that I believe that there *is* a God, and I was, in however clumsy and absurd a way, speaking on behalf of His honor, His hopes. And I was kept free from capture for a certain time to do a certain work, a work which had meaning to many people, a sign of hope. Then I was captured, and the next phase began. But I always knew that that time was parenthetical and that I was going to be spared nothing, neither jail nor anything else. I knew that there was a certain delay to do this work—period. And it might have gone on much longer, except for events that we now know of.

LL: Where did you go first, after your escape from the Seder?

DB: That night we went into the woods near Cornell. Very shortly thereafter, I established connection with Philip and, in spite of a considerable roadblock around the central New York area, I was able to rejoin him within a couple of days. Then we sat down for several days of rejoicing in being together again and of discussing where we were going from there, what this whole opportunity opened up. And there the discussion of Philip's planned surfacing at St. Gregory's Church came up. That was decided upon, and we separated again shortly before the scheduled day.

LL: Did Philip intend to give himself up at St. Gregory's?

DB: That wasn't the idea at all. He was going to make an appearance there and try to bow out again. But neither we nor our friends had any idea of the anger of the FBI after my Cornell disappearance or of the saturation of the area around St. Gregory's that night with agents. We had no way of knowing that. In retrospect it seems simple-minded that we didn't realize how serious things were. But at the time, we had no idea of the expenditure of FBI ego in our fate. We thought that they would probably take it easy for quite a while yet. As I said, we had only been underground for about two weeks. Then, too, there was an unpublicized agreement between the FBI and the pastor of St. Gregory's that no one would be touched, no attempt would be made to take Philip captive, until after that church service. And we made the utterly amazing decision to trust the FBI. Movement, take warning!

LL: And they caught Phil hiding in a closet?

DB: Yes.

LL: If Phil had been able to remain at large also, I suppose your real purpose was to form an underground together?

DB: Yes, that was very much our intention.

I would like to give a couple of examples of our growing understanding of the tactics of the FBI after that night. 1 was staying overnight in the city the night Phil was captured at St. Gregory's. The next morning, I was conveyed out at dawn. Lucky me! It was that very morning that the FBI began their search-and-destroy mission in the houses of various religious friends of ours. I got away from my overnight hostel by the space of about one half-hour. Of course, I didn't hear about this for a couple of days. But that, combined with Phil's capture in the rectory, brought home to me for the first time that the game was being played for keeps.

Then we learned, a little later, that FBI agents were sporting guns when they picked up George Mische and when they invaded the wedding of the Scoblicks looking for me. So growing over those next three weeks or so was a sense that this was a serious business indeed, that if I wanted to play the game I'd better do my best to make the terms of the game public for my own protection. Which I proceeded to do. Every time they appeared on my trail with guns, the public knew about it. I was very deliberate in bringing this out in my writing. And I'm sure it was an added embarrassment, because people were very interested in the fact that the FBI was using the tactics on priests and nuns that they had been using on blacks and students since Kent and Jackson State.

Well, to resume my story, I was in my next hideout for only about four days or so. And there I had another extremely narrow escape which I think it is instructive to talk about.

I was staying at the house belonging to relatives of a dear friend. The house was empty because the relatives were on vacation. One night, in the midst of preparations for supper—everything had gone very peacefully and we were recovering from Phil's capture—there came a sudden knock on the door. I was with a friend, luckily for me. So when there came this sudden, rather violent knocking, I hied myself upstairs, because that was the best place to listen without being seen. Over the balustrade, I could hear an infuriated voice demanding to know if I was in the house. And I slowly began to realize that the game was up, or very nearly up, with me. The invader was a relative of the owners who had evidently witnessed some comings and goings in the house. He had been reading the papers, had somehow concluded that I was in the house, and had come around in a fury.

At that point I simply went downstairs. There was no advantage in causing any further turmoil. He was white-faced and shaking, and he said something like, "You're Berrigan, aren't you?" I said, "Yes." And he pointed to the phone and said: "I give you two choices: either you pick up the phone and call the FBI, or I do." So I thought for a moment with a fatalism one gets skilled in, and then I said to him: "Well, I don't like your alternatives. I'll leave the house immediately." So I went upstairs to put my few traps into my sack, fully expecting that when I came down I would hear him on the phone with the FBI. He was not. And as we left the house there began to dawn on me the faint notion that perhaps he was bluffing, that he no more wanted the FBI in the house than I did, because of the involvement of his family, and maybe, I thought, we still had a small chance.

LL: Was he Catholic, by the way?

DB: Oh, sure.

LL: Is that why he was so angry?

DB: I think that had something to do with it. He was a veteran also, and that's often a lethal combination.

So we left. We had great difficulty getting out of town, because there seemed to be no cabs and no public conveyances, and I hid out in a movie house for about three hours watching Walt Disney's *Fantasia*, and expecting the house lights to go on any minute and the big search and seizure. But strangely, none of this happened.

That was a nightmarish evening. We spent hours and hours in between various buses and subways, trying to get in touch with friends. It seemed as though every phone in the metropolitan area was either out of order or busy, or else nobody was home. So we kept drifting in a Kafkaesque dream, by bus and subway and train and more bus again, toward New York, before we could get to a friend's house. So it was a long and bitter night.

But I think all these things were good, because they were reducing my illusions about the ease of survival. It seems to me that my near-capture also confronted certain people who were desperately frightened on the occasion of my appearance, but were forced at the same time to reshuffle their relationships very quickly and make decisions which I think they became thoughtful about and perhaps even ashamed of later.

LL: So in those first days you were really in flight, just keeping one step ahead of the law, and not taking the initiative. How did you get from the near-desperation involved in being a fugitive to the point of turning the situation around to your own advantage? How did you make contact with the kind of people who could help you do this?

DB: Well, my idea was to get in touch with a key person, and to get to a place remote enough so that my tail was not always under the cat's claw. Where I would have a little space to begin thinking and planning with one or two other people. And that's exactly what happened next. There was a change in the tempo of life, and for several days I was able to settle down and do some serious talking and thinking and meeting with friends, discussing the question: What does this mean, and where do we go from here?

LL: Can you give some idea of the daily routine you followed while you were underground?

DB: I had to adapt myself to the working day of the people that I was living with. That was usually a very good arrangement, because I was able to do a great deal of reading and writing and meditating during most of the day. I also walked abroad in season. I remember poignantly that I was being hunted during the most beautiful time of year, spring and summer.

An ordinary day would go like that. Then in the evening there would be meetings of one sort or another, at which any number of questions would come up—from the meaning of my presence in that particular group to the next public event, to arrangements for travel, to reports on work that people had been doing on my behalf. The evenings were strictly working sessions, along with the weekends, while the days generally belonged to me.

LL: As I remember, you arranged to have a series of meetings with groups of middle-class professionals. Why the emphasis on such people?

DB: I was always trying to get exposure to what other people were thinking—from leading academics who were somewhat connected with the movement to students, to blacks, to strict activists, resistance people themselves, people who either had been involved in jeopardy with the law or were about to embrace it. We had several very important meetings with such people. Obviously, the best meetings were those between myself and people in resistance, most of whom I already knew anyway. There was an immediate meshing of minds and hearts and plans and sharp discussion for long, long periods. On the other hand, it was dislocating to many of the liberal community to have me in their midst.

LL: You're talking about professors and academics?

DB: And student types. And even people who had been in early resistance actions but found that *this* thing was going too far. That was what I could read in their faces.

Maybe it would be a help to give a classic example of what I mean. There was a chaplain at one of our distinguished universities who had been quite prominent and visible as a friend of mine before I went underground. He was well known in his own right as a resistance figure. An overture was made to him through a third party that I be invited to preach on his precincts. And the proposal was quickly and definitively turned down. I was offered the rather meaningless alternative that I could appear at one of the services and take part in a dialogue *after* the service, which of course never appealed to me. I felt, very simply, that I had something to say to a whole community, and I wasn't going to undergo the jeopardy that would have been involved in order to appear merely as another member of that community, dialoguing with the chaplain instead of announcing the Word of God. I saw my function as speaking to the people about who I was and where I was, as I did later in a church in Philadelphia. So I was not about to undergo the jeopardy of that situation for the sake of catering to his fear.

LL: In other words, you saw your priestly function of announcing the Word of God and your political role as indissoluble?

DB: Right. I also felt that the chaplain's reaction took no account of our friendship. He was denying any possible continuity between my situation before going underground and his acceptance of me afterward. I decided that he was offering me this alternative in the desperate hope that I would find it so unattractive and minimal that I would be a fool to accept it.

Well, after that setback I was led to reevaluate things, and it was a long time before my friends and I again approached a church figure for any mutual project. We began to wait for some lead from them, rather than our making the approach. I thought it would be much more fruitful if they would come a certain distance in their own lives before approaching me. Whereas we would probably be bringing on the conniptions by suddenly appearing and suggesting a thing like this which was off their radar.

LL: I imagine it wasn't only the idea of your appearing that threw the fear of God into those people, but also the fact that when you did appear you challenged those whom you addressed to engage in acts of resistance that violated the law?

DB: Right. I think their fear was also connected with the fact that many people had had a bad experience in resistance, or in something approaching it. I got the feeling that many of them had *barely* come through their past. In other words, they hadn't come through it with enough resources for the next step, and now they were suddenly being asked to take that next step. And the old ghosts were abroad again, almost as they had been before they took their own first step. That is to say: "What's to happen to everything that I somehow have salvaged out of my life, out of court, out of indictments? I have those same nagging questions about my job, my security, my family, my future. I've saved things to this point and still done something, and now this guy wants to threaten everything again. And it's too much."

I don't want to get overly judgmental, but I suppose that every threat also contains an invitation. And maybe, in the case of those who are purportedly people of faith, it is an invitation which comes as a clue, an invitation which is not totally from man. And I felt that if they knew me well enough, if they had been my friends and had been open to what is essentially a moral continuum, that I was not asking too much. Ninety percent of the fears people conjure up are independent of the reality of the situation anyway. I know that from my own life.

LL: I'd like to get some sense of the interchange that you had with various families while you were a fugitive. It must have been extremely interesting for you, as a priest and as a celibate, to live in a family setting. I'm curious to know what reactions you had to an experience that must have been a very novel one for you, and whether you gained any new insights into the possibilities and problems of family life in our culture.

DB: I suppose what was best for me was a firsthand taste of the anguish and difficulties of family life today. I mean the money-grubbing for survival, the wear and tear on all parties by these close relationships, the fact that children of different ages have a way of invading and modifying and even assaulting their parents. And, vice versa, the skill and the clumsiness of parents in dealing with these very sensitive younger lives. All these things, which are bread and butter to parents and husbands and wives, were very new to me up close in that way.

It was also interesting that each family had to make room for me. I don't mean physically; I mean in their living space upstairs in their heads, in their perception of themselves and of one another. Because I was trying to come to them not merely as a star boarder or a prestige figure or a romantic adventurer who would be essentially parasitic on their existence and who would make no difference in the long run in the way they understood themselves in the world. Rather, I was deliberately trying to enter into situations where I could offer something new. And I had a sense that at times I even provoked things—discussions, criticisms, tensions.

LL: Was your criticism always well received?

DB: I think generally that, because I had awakened their trust, they were quite willing to discuss these things. The kinds of people who would take me in were not apt to look upon their children as sacred objects from outer space anyway. I think it was a very gentle kind of give-and-take, mostly. But there was also the vexing question, which I had first to understand and then, I think, to help them make explicit, of why children should be such an absorbing function or task for adults. Why they should presume to suck adults into such concern, such haste, such time consumption that there was so little left for other families of the world, especially the families of the war. And I think questions like these led into the deeper issues of whether or not the family as we knew it and were experiencing it could survive; or indeed whether it *deserved* to survive. We got into pretty deep waters on these things.

As I've said elsewhere—I guess it's nothing new—I see the American family bogged down in consumerism, socialized in its attitudes toward a war-making, destructive, racist society, helpless there, floundering about in its own monetary and social and sexual difficulties. Far short of any necessity, both men and women write off their creative potential because they are so exhausted by the projects of survival and by the task of keeping their children afloat. So the idea of a "movement family" is so extraordinarily rare as to be almost unheard of. Simply, I wanted to know why. I had certain suspicions as to why, but obviously these things had to be tested in lives and experiences, theirs and mine.

LL: And your conclusion was that the family unit as such must be broken up?

DB: As we know it. There have to be resisting families, just as there have to be resisting everything else. And one can't be exempted from this responsibility simply because his whole life belongs within a nest, you know?

LL: But granting that, are you attacking the unit of the family as such, or are you attacking the economic and political system which in our culture forces upon it these necessities that you find so all-consuming?

DB: I don't see how the two questions can be separated. The family as we know it is precisely the creation of the post-industrial society. By now the relationship between family and society is totally mutualized; the family as we know it cannot exist except by being parasitic on the culture and the economy, and vice versa. So it's a kind of vicious circle in which no one is thriving and the great questions are forever kept at distance.

LL: Can we shift our focus somewhat? Your critique of families raises another kind of question—this one is about you. I guess you must be aware that some people think that you are a little bit arrogant, or—

DB: —demented? (Laughs)

LL: (Laughing) Everybody knows you're demented.

DB: (Laughing) Right! Very good! Let's be precise.

LL: Seriously, though, many of your enemies and even some of your friends have criticized you for being impatient about other people's human shortcomings— especially those who offer you verbal support but have difficulty crossing the line between words and action. I think this kind of criticism was more common toward the beginning of your sojourn underground than it was toward the end. Which leads me to ask you if you think that your experience underground, sharing the lives of other people in such intimate relationships as you did, might not have made you more compassionate?

DB: I think that the difficulty you bring up is simply part of one's continuing education. It's always going to be important to a thoughtful person how others are reacting to him. And he cannot but take seriously the criticism of good people, thoughtful people.

To answer your question as applied to the underground, I think I would agree with you. That was a big hiatus in my former experience. I had always been an outsider to family life, except for very short periods. But underground I was living with families for a comparatively long time. From one point of view, I was at their mercy; and yet from another point of view there's nothing like living with other people to awaken instincts of compassion and to dull the edge of a criticism which is strictly an outsider's.

Now, I should add in all fairness that the matter which you bring up was part of a continuing difficulty in prison also. Many of the prisoners found Phil and myself very hard to deal with. It is not easy to be in a position where one is respected and looked up to because of his experience, because of his style; and where at the same time one is asked to step inside the skins and skulls of other people half his age who have been quite broken by almost every element of their background, from their marriage to their families to their prison experience. Such prisoners were trying desperately to clutch at something, but they hadn't gotten seriously to the building or the rebuilding of life itself. They were nonetheless desperately hoping that something would occur magically, maybe because of us. And then they found we were introducing rather unpopular and constant notions of discipline, honesty and unselfishness. We were demanding, for example, that class sessions of the discussion group we led in prison would go beyond sensitivity and a mutual licking of wounds into areas of content, of reading and pondering. This was all very new; they found it harsh, and they dropped away, most of them, over the long haul.

Obviously, there is little point in debating criticisms which are bound to be a continuing part of our lives. Phil and I are conscious that the demands we make on other people must first of all be made on ourselves. And these demands must be muted and controlled by our overriding compassion, our sense of the way people are broken on the wheel of modern life in this society, and the fact that goodness speaks to goodness, but abstract principles don't get far. Do you know what I mean? And, well, we tried to be men with the men, but it was only trying.

LL: Perhaps the process of trying helped you to be more of a man too.

DB: I hope so. Or less of an un-man, at least.

LL: Have you ever looked back on your period underground and wished that you had done some things differently, or better?

DB: Well, I don't usually indulge in the kind of reverie that wastes time in regretting mistakes, either in myself or others. I think we made a lot of mistakes, but I think they were inevitable.

LL: Tactical mistakes?

DB: Yes. And also maybe a mistaken understanding of what was the best to do at a given moment. Maybe that was a failure in self-understanding, too.

LL: Did you see your main purpose in going underground as an effort at public relations?

DB: Public education, perhaps, as it turned out. Though I think there are other kinds of underground that have very different tactics in mind. But I don't think I could be a part of that.

LL: For example?

DB: Like disappearing indefinitely, for example. I would have retorted: Why not be in jail if you only want to disappear?

LL: Do you think now that you should have tried to do a little more organizing of the people around you, in order to build a movement or at least something that would survive your capture?

DB: I think maybe Phil would have, but I don't think I could. Then again, he would not have been able to do many of the things I did. Which is to say that we're very different; complementary, but very different. But I think he would have been much tougher as an organizational person that I was.

LL: Or more thoughtful about leaving something behind? That's really what I'm asking you. I mean, it seems to me that you were very much caught up in what you were doing, the relationships you were forming, the things that *you* were learning and experiencing, and especially in the effort to deal with the press; and that you weren't giving much thought to the question: Now, is there a finite point at which I will no longer be part of this, when people won't be able to depend on me any more, and when their excitement won't come out of my presence or the thrill of harboring me? And, when that time comes, will there still be something going on? Will these same people stay together to take care of others who go underground or to work in other ways below surface?

DB: It seems to me that accomplishing that goal would have required moving with very different people than I did. What you are talking about, by implication at least, is resistance communities.

LL: Isn't that really what you were trying to form among the people you were living with?

DB: We talked a lot about it, but I don't think that in that short time the thing really took hold. They were family people; and by and large resistance communities don't develop in middle-class professional family life.

LL: But haven't you yourself often said that until you get middle-class professional family people moving in the direction of resistance, you don't have anything going?

DB: Yes. Well, all I could say is that I tried, I guess. Even then, how do you evaluate these things? Maybe one could say: Well, I just wasn't around long enough. Or one could say: Well, I just didn't work at it hard enough. Or one could say: It was in the air, but they didn't take to it.

LL: Well, perhaps three and a half months is no time

at all in which to get anything of that magnitude started. You only begin to make an impression. Yet even in that short time, from all I've heard and read, you made a forceful impression on many of the individuals with whom you came in contact. This leads me to ask if now, looking back, you think you may have devoted too much of your energy and time underground to dealing with the press and educating the public, and not enough time to developing resistance communities?

DB: Everything's limited, you know. I don't have the impression that a great amount of time was given to newspaper interviews. They came up once a week at most. Meanwhile, I was writing like a fiend myself, which I think was equally important.

You see, being entirely dependent upon others to set up the simplest meeting with another person, let's say—whether media or nonmedia person—made matters very difficult. It was not just a matter of walking out into the street or picking up a phone and saying, "I want to get to somebody about resistance." We had a lot of serious meetings about resistance, but they were all bloody difficult to set up. And they required a hell of a lot of time on people's parts. I mean, I couldn't push people any further.

LL: A number of people have criticized you for being a kind of "media freak" during that time. I suppose that is because your image in the press while you were underground was mainly that of a jazzy Robin Hood who was bouncing around from one surprise appearance to another, one step ahead of the law, with no more serious purpose than freaking out the FBI.

DB: First of all, I would be very interested in seeing any comparable literature out of that period. I would like to match it with my writings, as well as with our serious discussions of the issues of that summer and of the war itself.

But I don't want to get deadly about it or merely defensive. I would also say that it seems to me that the only people who have a right to play around, to celebrate, are those whose lives stand somewhere. And once it is clear that games, play, festivals proceed from self-assurance, from one's sense of being himself, then—I love to play! So I make no apologies to the mortician culture for playing around a bit and for having the guts to make a life game out of the death game my pursuers were in fact promoting. One of the most sorrowful features of life today is that people can't associate a kind of overflow of good humor and joy with the struggle. So the whole of life in the long run becomes extremely depressing and discouraging. People surrender to the sense that their racy feelings, their joyous overflow are forbidden games, somewhat as in an earlier time it was forbidden for children to prattle or laugh in church. You know, I wrote poetry in jail. I guess that's the most concrete way of saying what I'm trying to say.

In a sense it was much easier for me to retain those feelings and to be true to them underground than it was in jail, where the difficulties of confinement had immediate repercussions on my health and I found myself for months kind of dragging around. But underground I remember a priest asking me once how I could bear the psychological pressure, and I said to him: "I never felt any, I never felt any." And I was glad that my adversaries *did*, because that was one way of explaining the difference between us.

Now could we speak a little bit about my relationship to the media? This might be useful.

I thought of these activities as a continuation of

teaching. Everything in my background led me to believe that it was important, a skill that made me responsible to others. I never made an appearance in any form of the media that I had to be ashamed of afterward as being marked by a superficiality or a levity that wasn't befitting the people I was speaking for, especially the Vietnamese. All of us carefully thought out everything I wrote and every appearance I made on television. I was always deeply aware of the risks involved, and we determined to go ahead because we thought it was the best way to pose the thoughtful questions that would induce change in others or in ourselves. My feelings about such work are no different now. I guess the only debate that should seriously continue is whether or not my public appearances were a factor in making the pursuers more resolute about getting me. I'm quite sure that I exasperated them continually. But that was something that we tried to weigh at the time. And, as it turned out, these appearances were not decisive in my being captured anyway.

LL: I was going to ask you about that. I guess you're quite aware of the reason for your capture on Block Island. Your presence there was given away by Sister Elizabeth McAlister in letters she wrote to your brother, letters which were intercepted by the FBI. I wonder how you felt when you finally understood how you had been flushed out?

DB: Well, I think my feeling was a mild sense of relief. The question had long ceased to be an important one, except as a matter of closing off one period of my life. And of closing off a number of rather wounding speculations that had been going on among my friends.

LL: About how you had been given away?

DB: Yes, and about certain failures that we thought

perhaps had occurred. Everyone of course was speculating with great fervor at the time, and the wildest rumors were circulating. Certain people within our circle were even accused of lapses of vigilance. So I was happy that the question was closed, that it was a simple matter of, let's say, a rather imprudent reference to myself and my friends, and nothing more.

Now, I'm sure that if this thing had gone another ten months it would have hit another speed. That's undeniable. But I don't even know how fruitful it is to speculate on all these things. Suppose I had said to my friends: "Look, I don't want to meet any more media people; I just want you to set up personal meetings with promising professionals." First of all, that would have been as difficult for them as what they were doing. You simply can't do it every night of the week, physically speaking. You can't get that many people together in that time. If we set up two really serious meetings a week, that was the limit of those who were working on it. And we did that. Moreover, on our rides across the seaboard we also met with a lot of people who had serious intentions. But it was always extraordinarily risky.

I guess I don't go in for this sort of speculation and evaluation of the past unless I'm really pushed to it. I mean I'm much more Zen about it all. Which is not meant to defend anything; it's just the way I am.

What I would say finally about the whole experience is that it was solid gold, that it was the best I could do at the time. And whenever Phil and I talked about it, he was delighted about the way it had gone. I think it's because he knew me, because he knew my limitations and my gifts as well. He used to say that my underground was the only exciting thing in all that time, in all those doldrums between Kent State and my capture. And I feel very good about it.

I think in this question we're trying to discuss lies a deep and lasting difference between ourselves as the Catholic Left and most other phases of the movement. This struck me again recently in talking with Rennie Davis. I think that as the war goes on people are more and more obsessed by the necessity of delivering results, of efficiency. To me the imperative is debased. Or it is drawn from the instinctual world of animals, or from artifacts of man, engineering products. I prefer to insist on the deep cultural or religious resources that remind us: We cannot induce change until we have undergone change. Practically speaking, this sense of things has always issued in a common agreement between Phil and myself that some sort of spiritual retreat was the necessary prelude to some new tactic, and not vice versa.

In a recent press conference I was again faulted for not having a program, for God's sake—something I haven't had for years, and in fact never will have. I suggested that the weary, repetitive groove of the rhetoric of the sixties, which I heard again at that press conference, means that people's minds are "geared," are unfree, in this terrifying engineered sense we've spoken of, instead of being plunged into life forces, in touch with their past, their soul and their community.

2

LEE LOCKWOOD: Why do you call the Danbury Penitentiary a "popsicle prison"?

DANIEL BERRIGAN: Well, because every aspect of the life there is enervating, rather than openly vicious or wounding in a physical sense. It amounts to a dislocation of the human spirit without a great measure of overt cruelty. And then, also, I meant to suggest the idiot, low-grade distractions that are available there: skin flicks and violence flicks every weekend; a library for which they have never bought a periodical or a book; the wretched religion that lazes along with the current; the grievous fact that so many of the prisoners resign themselves to the place as a continuing distraction from life rather than a means of putting their lives together. And that's exactly what the management wants. If a prisoner can be wired for sound eighteen hours a day and wander about with absurd things happening inside his head, then he's a prisoner indeed, in the worst possible sense.

One of the sorrowful things I'll remember for a long time is the vapidity that infects even a very intelligent prisoner at times. The mind flakes out into his family or his past or his home, and he gets lost in that reverie, lost to what is going on around him. And that went on for rather long periods in some cases, a kind of amnesia or twilight sleep. But finally, a person chooses to pull himself back with a start to the job of having to face what is before him. I experienced that myself at times. Unless you are very disciplined, you can drown in a kind of dream-world. And especially for people who are not equipped to read and to reflect and who need their fantasies spruced up, prison is a very wounding time.

In the beginning, merely to cope was a tremendous project. I found the first three months a kind of personal death. Certain parts of me simply couldn't be active any more; certain talents had to be put on ice. A certain edge of my sensibility, my imagination, was rusted by the routine, by the fact that there was so little stimulus, by the fact that I was living in a vacuum. This was very rough. And then I had to say to myself, at some point, "Let it die; let it all go, and concentrate on whatever you can bring to birth again, whatever you can get reborn." It was much more of a Zen project than I had ever been involved in before. Like every free man, I'd always been able to follow the lodestone of my own inclinations and to develop my talents in an unfettered way: to travel, to speak, to be constantly challenged. In prison, of course, that was impossible.

That's the simplest way and least rhetorical way I

know to put it: You really accept death as a fact, in all the subtle hellish modes that a place like that opens up, because the prison is expert in all the ways of putting men to death. But if you can do that, then something new emerges, I think, and you survive. That's the discovery I was able to make.

LL: What was the greatest deprivation that prison life imposed upon you? What did you miss the most?

DB: Hmmm. It's very hard to say, you know, because everything is all really one: it's freedom. Freedom in regard to your friends, in regard to nature. Those are the two that occur to me right away; and then, right on the heels of that, freedom in regard to all modes of self-expression.

LL: You weren't allowed to write poems or articles?

DB: Well, all those things were subject to idiotic rules and overseeing and threat of confiscation. It was repressive rehabilitation at its damnedest.

LL: I'd like to get a picture of what your daily routine was like in prison. Where did you live, where did you work, that sort of thing?

DB: To start off with, we were all put through an initiation ceremony which went on for a couple of weeks and is common to all federal prisons and I suspect all state ones as well. It has to do with the effort to get one acquainted with the routine of the prison. New prisoners are ordinarily segregated and have talks by guards, chaplains, heads of education, and various other functionaries in charge of work and recreation and food, and religion. So one stews there for a couple of weeks, getting over his initial sense of shock. We had a certain access to other prisoners during that time, but were strictly watched and regulated.

Then, after those two weeks, we were let loose into

the general fray. After a purported interview with three or four of the bureaucrats—an interview which, like most personal exchanges there, was totally without meaning—we were assigned jobs, again purportedly on the basis of some prior experience or skill. At that point we began really to live the life of prisoners. I was assigned first to the common living quarters in the dormitory.

LL: You had dormitories instead of cells?

DB: Right. And then shortly thereafter, I guess within a couple of months, I was reassigned to a kind of modified cellblock, which was supposed to be a little bit easier and quieter. But in reality it was almost worse than the original situation, because we were in the same building as the "holdover" and the solitary units, "the hole." Those in solitary had no work assignments and were locked in their cells all day. So they were free to raise hell all during the night, which made it very hard for the rest of us.

LL: What kind of room were you in?

DB: They were cells without windows which gave on a general block and a long series of windows that could be opened, but not by us, and a kind of catwalk in front of each of these cellblocks. I think there were four floors of them, about fifteen cells to a floor.

LL: But only one person to a cell?

DB: Yes, single cells. But all night long the place reverberated like a drum from the hell-raising in the cellblocks opposite us. The homosexuals were also segregated on the first floor of this block, and of course they tended to form a group that was noisy and determined to make itself heard. So it was very rough. I was there about four months, and it was there that I began to feel most acutely the really rough aspects of prison: the lack of privacy and quiet. Because any time you were in there, except after the general lockup at night, you were subject to visits from anyone who might be passing by. All the doors were open until eleven at night.

LL: How big was your cell?

DB: It was about enough for a bed and a sink and a toilet and a locker, accouterments common to all the prisoners. That was about it. Maybe six by eight or nine feet—something like that.

LL: Was it considered a privilege to have your own cell instead of living in a dormitory like most of the other prisoners?

DB: There were smaller numbers of people in these private quarters, I guess maybe one-third of the whole populace. You became eligible for these as you gained your so-called good time. Then, after four or five months in there, I changed quarters again into one of the so-called "honor houses," which contained what were actually individual rooms with their own doors. These doors were locked only at night. It was a good deal quieter and more private there. The disadvantage was that here there was no visiting from the other houses, so you found yourself a little cut off from the general run of new arrivals. But the question for Phil and me was how to build something within whatever housing unit we were living and of really getting to know the men there.

LL: You and Phil were both at Danbury for eighteen months. Did you room together?

DB: No, in the whole time we were there, we were never assigned to the same housing unit, which I think was deliberate. But we were able to be together at meals and during the recreation periods, so there was never any real hardship. In fact, it might have been a good idea.

) 40 (

Living in different parts of the compound, we were able to mingle with different people.

LL: What about at night? Could you visit from one dormitory to the other?

DB: No, that was never allowed. You could be arrested for what they called "inter-house visiting." That was their way of cutting down on the drug trade and the homosexual trade; but from our point of view they were cutting down on our sharing resistance ideas.

LL: Did they split up the resisters too?

DB: In general, everybody began in the dorms and then graduated as we did to these "honor houses." But the younger resisters were segregated in the sense that they didn't usually make these houses; if they did, it was only toward the end of their terms. *We* made them, but I think it was one way for them to dispose of us. It was a great advantage for us, because it gave us the privacy to study and to prepare our classes. In general, life was much less intolerable in these places. So, given everything, it was not the worst arrangement in the world.

It was very helpful for us to be able to meet with the prisoners in an atmosphere removed from the tremendous noise and turmoil of the other houses. Each of us had study groups going in the houses we were living in.

LL: What sort of study groups?

DB: Over the whole period of our term, we met with a small number of inmates after the general lockup from nine to eleven P.M., at least two nights a week. As I recall, Phil's group was more loose. My group was generally studying St. Matthew's gospel. I think we spent about ten months on that. Then for a long period also, we tried something more flexible. Each member came in with some fifteen- or twenty-minute rap about his reading or his life or his interests or something that had happened to him, and the rest of us took up the discussion from there.

LL: How many people were in your group?

DB: There were never more than four, because it was never feasible in one room with more.

LL: And this was allowed by the authorities?

DB: Yes, they didn't bother you after the lockup. You could be either in the television room, or in someone's room, or writing letters or reading in your own room. There was a hack around, but he never made any big deal out of this.

LL: You mentioned that the homosexuals were segregated at Danbury. Were they given the same privileges of visiting in each other's rooms and so on?

DB: Only within their house, like everyone else. This house was called something like "modified discipline"— I think that was the name for it. Because they had people in solitary, those who had been to the kangaroo court, and because the homosexuals lived there, there was more surveillance in that house and you were liable to more trouble if there was any kind of noisy gathering at all. But in general the homosexuals moved as they wanted to, and they found a general acceptance among the prisoners, I would say.

At the same time, they took a good deal of hassling by the authorities. In fact, they were the most openly persecuted group in the prison because of the straight, very narrow-minded guards and because of the mentality of the place. And they were the only ones who were not subject to even the pretense of "rehabilitation." The attitude of the authorities toward them was: either leave them alone if you were mild and decent; or keep hassling them and fooling with them if you were sadistic or if you had homosexual tendencies yourself, as many of the guards did. Fool around with them, and keep them moving.

LL: Is homosexuality a problem at Danbury as it seems to be in prisons where security is higher?

DB: The problem, as far as I am concerned, was that the homosexuals were not really aware of themselves in a way that made any difference. They hadn't become politicized at all, and it was only very much toward the end of my stay that I got a sense that they were coming together at all. Short of that, they were playing their own games, which I think were useless and childish. They were generally retarded in their development, and that left them very open to the games that the authorities and guards wanted to play. And that was too bad. But it reflected the situation in the other communities there, because the blacks and the Puerto Ricans were not getting into much either.

LL: At Danbury, there wasn't the problem of heterosexuals becoming homosexuals because of the sexual deprivation of prisons?

DB: Oh, there was a certain edge of that, but it never became important. It was a laughing matter for some and a matter of indifference to most others. The homosexuals were always available to any kind of fringe people who wanted that kind of play. That was clear. But there wasn't the hard ploy toward young prisoners that's part of the more security-minded prisons. A young prisoner coming to Danbury, especially a young resister, found no special difficulty if he was not stupid himself, because there were always friends who would help him. And even among the staff, especially in the hospital, there

) 43 (

were good people who would help in any crisis, defending a prisoner or even urging him to fight things out, which was sometimes necessary.

LL: What about drugs? A lot of the kids in Danbury are up for drug abuse, right?

DB: Use and abuse. And dealing.

LL: Was there a drug traffic going on inside prison?

DB: Yes, there were drugs constantly coming and going. And in all sorts of ways, one of which of course was through the visiting room itself. But through other sources as well.

LL: Including the guards?

DB: I would say that was rare, but it happened too. The idea of prosecuting anybody for contraband letters or periodicals became more and more ridiculous in the light of what was happening day after day. It was one of the easiest things in the world to go to the visiting room to collect a delivery, or to arrange it through somebody who was working outside. Also, the penalties were so remote that those who came in under drug charges and decided they wanted to continue their thing could find a way of doing it that was not at all threatening.

LL: They weren't penalized if they were caught with drugs?

DB: They were penalized if they were caught, but the number who were caught was so utterly small in relation to the number who were using, buying, selling and dealing that the threat was meaningless.

LL: And the penalties were administrative rather than judicial?

DB: Well, it depended. There were two or three serious legal cases while I was there, cases that went into criminal courts outside. It seemed extremely arbitrary on what occasions they decided to prosecute and on what occasions they didn't. It was very hard to figure out, but I suspect some of it had to do with a kind of spasm that arose on occasion, when they decided they'd better make an example of somebody because things were getting out of hand. But things had a way of getting back to normal rather quickly.

LL: What did you do during the day? What was your work routine?

DB: I found from the beginning that the whole notion of work was a really astonishing up-front factor in the mentality of those who were running the prisons. You know, before I went to jail, when I thought abstractly of prisons or if I were asked to construct a prison imaginatively, I would never have thought of prisoners as being required to work. But it makes sense in a weird way when you think about it. How else are you going to keep people from mischief, from thoughtfulness, from community, from further crimes, from everything good and bad that might happen to men in an enforced and false situation?

But I must say I always felt a kind of wonderment at the sound of the huge buzzer that routed people to work every morning. It was almost like a huge "raspberry" in honor of the Victorian English Protestant ethic. It declared to prisoners, day after day and month after month and year after year: "You'd better get with it, or else." And "getting with it" wasn't just lining up in lock step; it was going out to do something that declared you were useful or you were necessary or you were human, or that you had better *believe* all these things.

It was at that point of the day that the classical slouching, slow procession of sorrow and loss, all those illustrations that one has in his mind out of Goya and Daumier and Dickens, began to come true. As the prisoners moved toward their terrible, enforced, useless labor, so connected with the horror of the beginnings of the Industrial Revolution and child labor and long hours in the mines, all that era that preceded the unions, the organized, more humane labor—it was at that point that the full impact of the prison came home to you like a kick in the groin.

And it was at that point, in the sight of that movement toward work, that one had to decide his own attitude toward work and prison all over again: whether or not he would join that procession in the deadly depressed spirit that set it in motion, or whether he had some reason to go there in another spirit—with a lifted head and a smile and an eye for the other prisoners; with the conviction that, come what may, and whatever orders were given, *he was not going to be a slave.* He might go to work because he had other reasons for being there, but he wouldn't go in *their* spirit, because their spirit was a demand that one accept being in prison at all.

In other words, if one could lounge around in his living quarters all day, or if one could stay out in the sun all day, he would be much less a prisoner, because at least he would be choosing how to pass time—fooling around, wasting time, joking with others, kidding and gaffing. But because he was forced into the factory at that hour, five days a week and for overtime at certain periods of the year, he became a prisoner-slave. The obligation of work colored one's time sense; it colored one's sense of others; it gave a slavish taste to the day that was about to open and to the day that was about to close as he came back. It lent a certain rightness to the clothes he was forced to wear, because they were a kind of slave's clothing, made for work only. It regulated his day in a way that denied him space for joy or development or leisure or reading, all the things he might do as a free man. Or might *come* to do as a free man. A lot of people wouldn't, of course.

I never really quite got over that. That buzzer sounded at many other times of the day, but it never sounded with that kind of inhuman insistence as it did at eight in the morning. That might have been peculiar to me, in a sense, because I had always been on a very different time schedule, so it was a particular dislocation for me to start out for anything at that hour of the morning. I mean, I never quite made it. For years before I went to jail, I almost never got up before nine or nine-thirty or ten, depending on the night before. I think that people who are masters of their own existence or who live on campuses, students included, tend to be afternoon, evening, and late-into-the-night people. Even before that, as a writer, I had always been a night person.

LL: What time did you have to get up in prison?

DB: Well, I always skipped breakfast, so I would get up about seven-thirty and make myself a cup of oatmeal in my room and go to work from there.

LL: What time was breakfast for other prisoners?

DB: Breakfast went from about six-thirty to about seven-fifteen, every day but Sunday. Sunday was a two-meal day. There was a brunch between about nine-thirty to eleven and then a supper from four until five-thirty.

LL: Four o'clock is awfully early to be eating supper. Was it later on weekdays?

DB: No, it was always around the same time. You see, this order of the day guaranteed, first of all, that prisoners were counted by five P.M., and that the personnel who came in from outside had their work finished so that they could get a good evening at home. They could be out of the place by five-thirty or six at the latest, even the cooks.

) 47 (

Then your long evening was up to you. And for most people it was a desperately long evening. Imagine, if everybody was out of the dining hall by five P.M., and the lights didn't go out until eleven, we had six long, long hours to dispose of, especially in the winter. And most people didn't read, so that those hours were just a form of vegetation: television, playing cards, et cetera.

The TV rooms were always crowded. There was also a good deal of rapping among the younger people. A few of them had guitars, of course. There was at least one movie a week, which played on Friday night, on Saturday noon and Saturday evening—the same movie. Then, when the Jaycees became a big force in the place, they were able to get another movie. So on most weekends toward the end there were two.

Those of us who seldom watched television ordinarily found the weekend movie a very important relief. And occasionally, when they would show a decent one, the word got around quickly and there was great rejoicing. Those movies also were a very peculiar experience, especially in the beginning. One sat there looking at this wide screen, this tremendous outpouring of the culture, very seductive, usually. The theme was nearly always either skin or violence, but now and again there were some very beautiful shots or sequences dealing with nature or so many other things that were forbidden to us. And one could cruelly and acutely see himself in that scene, on those paths, by that ocean, in those mountains, could see horizons that were lost to sight, faces that were lost . . . and one gravitated back and forth between that screen and where he was stuck. One sensed his own misery as well as the very deep sensual anguish around one.

There was a group of younger prisoners who used to

come to two or three showings of the same movie, to see some highly charged sexual scene, and then leave again. Those were terrible moments for anybody who could understand, without moralizing, why those poor guys were reaching out to plastic, disembodied sex, or whatever it was, on the screen. There was nothing in the prison which had such meaning for large numbers of young prisoners, whether it was good food—which was rare—or religion, or education, or rapping, or music. The most immediate thing was the sight of another body, especially if it was naked. And the activity that that body was capable of, and their frenzy to be joined to it in some way. Well, that was a very sad measure of the abnormality of the scene, and also, of course, a metaphor of human deprivation in every respect.

LL: I used to sense that very poignantly and vividly when I visited you and Phil in the visiting room, and we'd be surrounded by writhing couples in various positions of sexual foreplay, striving for that kind of human contact so full of anguish and without fulfillment.

DB: Yes. But at least this was one prison where prisoners were allowed to touch their loved ones, where there wasn't a screen or a glass between them—a kind of mutual aquarium. But even there, you know, prison constantly brought home to one his deprived and dehumanized state as a human being.

What most visitors didn't know—at least they never knew it unless the prisoner told them—was that immediately after such a visit, many of us were subjected to a strip search. And I saw so often its impact upon the younger prisoners, when they would come out of a high with someone they loved and then were stripped to the bone in the next room; and this not a half-hour after the visit, but *immediately* afterward. That is, they

) 49 (

were immediately being reminded that they were nothing more than a piece of meat available for inspection.

And that was the price of having a visit at all—that was the way you came out. To walk out of the visitors room with a smile on your face and an inner glow because you had just shared at least some measure of love, and then to go into that utter denial of your humanity and of what had just taken place between two or three persons was a species of degradation that was, I would say, memorable. A memorable incursion of the state against the human being. Search, that is, and destroy. I would say that there were two things that were most difficult for most prisoners. One was coming out of the visiting room to the strip search. And the other was the threat that always overlay your mail and your letters.

LL: They were all read by prison officials?

DB: Yes, depending on the guard who was censoring that week. Most weeks, you could be sure there was very strict censorship. Again, it was almost like a delayed fuse placed under the prisoner's bed or in his cell. He could indulge in a certain reverie while writing a letter, almost as he did at a visit or after a visit, about something very intimate and important to him. And I so often had the experience that a prisoner would come out after writing a long letter and want to read it to me or to share it with me in summary. Then I would meet the prisoner a day or two later, after that same letter had been thrown back at him because some idiot guard had seen something objectionable in it and decided that it couldn't be sent out. It was a species of punishment that was very complex, because it involved the effort, obviously, to destroy a relationship, but also an equally cruel effort to make him unsteady or unclear about his own emotional moods so that he could never know, after a good feeling, how a bad feeling would be forced upon him. So that he would tend to become distrustful about getting into a good mood about other people, because maybe a letter, a labor of love, was going to be shoved back into his face, forbidden, a day or two later. This kept people off balance even in sane emotional responses to human beings.

LL: And I imagine that the longer they went without human contact with the outside world, the less certain they could be as to what was the right or wrong response on a given occasion.

DB: Well, that depended on the prisoner. There were other prisoners who opted for a minimum of visiting or letter writing because these punishments were so cruel. They just decided that to do a steadier kind of time was the best thing for them; not to have to undergo the risk of emotional loss and punishment. And then, of course, there were also prisoners who never had anyone to write to and whom no one ever visited; that was another kind of time.

LL: This sort of dehumanization seems totally at odds with the established concept of what prison is supposed to be—mainly rehabilitative; that is, aiming toward more humanity, toward integration into society. The kind of pressures and tortures you've described would tend to dehumanize and to isolate prisoners, to make them *less* human, *less* rehabilitated, I would think; less able to be integrated into society when they finally get out.

DB: Well, the story is the same from every prison, I guess, since the beginning. It certainly is true from every prison in our time. Every element which should be devoted to the rebuilding of human life or to its enhancing becomes a weapon against human beings in prison. And that by a very cruel and vindictive and deliberate will.

) 51 (

It's almost like the difference between, let's say, an automobile which is functioning well and one whose inner workings have suddenly gotten out of control. Where everything within the car suddenly becomes a menace to life, you know; you get the same runaway, nightmarish feeling about a place like Danbury. Nothing is working; and it's not because anything has accidentally gone wrong, but because over a long period of time people have become accustomed to using human institutions against human beings. And this is the triumphant end of it all—the prison.

LL: Do you see this sort of torture as a uniform policy of the Bureau of Prisons that is articulated by the wardens of individual prisons, a series of orders and instructions given to the guards, or do you see it as a matter of involuntary collaboration by the guards and other prison officials in an atmosphere of inhumanity?

DB: I don't know. I think that after a while, every institution, whether we're talking about the Church or a university or a prison, in varying degrees develops its own momentum which carries the individuals within it along with it, almost like a huge avalanche. They are simply destroyed by the downhill course of things. This process is slower in some institutions, where it is retarded by a kind of humanism that introduces other elements. But in a prison it is totally unmitigated and untouched by outside influences.

In other institutions of society, the university for example, there would be many mitigating factors against the destruction of human beings, obviously. In the Church also. But suppose elements of education and religion have become subservient to the general direction of the prisons? Then education and religion are subsumed in a way that makes them elements of degrada-

) 52 (

tion. They no longer have any independent voice, any kind of humane direction, at all.

I remember reading while I was in prison a statement by Jane Kennedy, a nurse who spent a lot of very hard time in jail in Chicago after burning draft files there. She said that the greatest difficulty for her in prison was to fight her hatreds. And I would say, amen.

Religion! I remember coming out on the compound on Sunday mornings after mass—after *mass*, mind you—with Phil and some of the others, and being so choked with hatred at what had gone on in there, the inane preachments, the contempt for suffering—well, you simply walked it out and kept quiet until you got your equilibrium back. Because everything your life outside had tried for, at least around the Eucharist, to prepare a space in which people could be human and in which aspects of generosity and goodness and acceptance were in the air—no matter what you had had to put up with in your life, you always had that. If you didn't have it for yourself, you had it to create for others. But in prison you had neither. And you went in there and put up with that thing.

Strangely enough, it wasn't anger about work or about food or about strip searches that used to get to me; it was anger about the Sunday morning mass. And I guess we felt that particular form of outrage because of everything our religion was supposed to stand for.

LL: Did you celebrate mass while you were in prison?

DB: Most of the time we were there, Phil and I were forbidden to celebrate with the other prisoners. They didn't want us in the position of being able to speak with others, of being able to interpret the gospel in ways that we thought were called for. So we would end up taking turns serving at the mass of this poor preacher.

) 53 (

He was a man who was able to reduce the message of Christ to the consistency of the food we ate all week— Elmer's Glue. The same awful, odorless, tasteless, sexless, passionless combo that you picked up on your tray, you also tasted on Sunday mornings in his sermons and also in his attitude, his laziness, his cowardice, his unwillingness to face the suffering that was eating at the rest of us all the time. What a skill he had at leading two lives: coming and going in a beautiful air-conditioned car, while keeping an office that was desolate and flybitten and dusty, where even the flag of the United States was rotten, where there wasn't a decent book, where there was no relief for anybody. I dwell upon this because it was a particular source of anger, as I say, and because we ourselves saw so clearly, because of our background, what could have been done by one courageous man in his position. The fact that he was a chaplain was secondary in a sense; but I think we felt particularly undone because the chaplain refused to be a man for others.

LL: Was the same true of all of the chaplains?

DB: Well, there were only two of them, plus a Jewish chaplain who came in on weekends. But among the three they varied only in the degree of their consciousness of being renegades of their tradition. All three were renegades, to any objective view.

It might be worthwhile to draw an analogy between the chaplain in prison and the chaplain in the armed forces. Among Catholics, at least, the question of the militarization or paramilitarization of religion came much to the fore in the last year or so that I was in prison, and the same question is bound to extend to the chaplaincies in jails in the years ahead. I am reminded of something Camus said about not so much seeking a world in which murder will not occur as seeking a world in which murder will not be legal. And I think in the same sense one should try to modify his goals with regard to the infection of religion by military practices. That is to say, one is not seeking chaplains who will help end murder in the army, or prison chaplains who will help bring down the prisons—that would be an immodest goal! But one *is* seeking, realistically here and now, chaplains who will at least be attuned to the daily cruelties and indignities visited upon prisoners, and who will stand, at least in the most acute cases, on the prisoners' side. That kind of witness is so rare in any prison that one would have welcomed any evidence of humanity like manna. But the manna never fell.

LL: It seems to me that, in large part, the various indignities which the prison system inflicts on prisoners may be due to the essential need that officials feel to keep the prison running with the fewest hitches. That is, to keep the machine well-oiled and running with the least amount of trouble. If so, prison officials would probably tend to choose chaplains who would cause the fewest problems among the men, who would be the most efficient in keeping the machine going.

DB: Yes, I would agree. Chaplains must run with the whole momentum of the system. In that way, it's very much like the army. In fact, it draws upon the army method of advancement. One doesn't just come into the prison system at any point of authority; he rises through the ranks. Most of these chaplains, especially the ones with most clout, have had either military experience or prison experience over a long period of time, so that they're acculturated to the whole scene. It's very hard in any case to single out these elements of cruelty versus carelessness or routine. The fact is that at the receiving end they add up to the same thing, a gross conglomeration of inhuman practice.

LL: But how do such practices continue, granted that a decent society is interested in conducting decent prisons?

DB: My difficulty with your question is that it presupposes that there's some sort of public debate in progress about better or worse ways of dealing with "criminals." But there isn't any debate at all. There isn't any public interest. And it's out of just this kind of historical disinterest of religion and of the intellectual community that the prison system has arisen. With an assist, of course, from the Quakers, those simple-minded reformists who decided that it was better that people be incarcerated with the Bible than that they suffer amputation or some sort of physical cruelty.

But I think that the history of prisons bears out the fact that periodic waves of interest follow upon periodic massacres such as that at Attica. There's always been a reformist movement after an outbreak, and reformism, in principle and at present, is separated from the larger questions of the society. I think Ramsey Clark and Dr. Menninger follow this trend unconsciously but exactly. That is, they are interested in ways of making prison more humane. But it's rare indeed to find a treatment of the question that goes into prison as a reflection of the general societal state of things, that asks questions such as, What is a prison anyway? Do we dare consider whether or not the very conception of prison as such is antihuman and counterproductive? Do we dare consider the possibility that such places can never work, no matter how they are frosted over with the latest psychological theories or the latest drug theories or the latest

Esalen theories? That they can't work because they are reflections of a society's will to punish its least protected members?

The opposite of prisons wouldn't ideally be such centers as we see growing in California and in New York; that is, drug centers or therapy centers or, at the other end of the spectrum, super–high-security jails. The opposite of the prisons is very hard for people to conceive of—even for prisoners, who have always regarded prisons as part of the picture. When I was in Danbury, one of the most striking things about the discussions that went on *about* prisons was the acceptance by the prisoners themselves of their condition. Many of them would declare that, whether in Cuba or in Sweden or in Russia or in China or here, there must be prisons, and that for men to be in prison is a natural condition of things. "We *should* be here. We *should* be working this thing out by being punished for it." And it was very hard to get them to see that they were saying much more about themselves than about the prisons.

LL: You were talking about prisoners watching movies and seeing these outdoor vistas denied to them. Are the prisoners at Danbury not allowed to go outdoors at all?

DB: Well, we had a little yard. You could go out there at any time during the day on Sundays and Saturdays, and you could be out there in the late afternoon and evening on ordinary days. But of course there was nothing to see except literally the four walls of the prison and, within it, in season, a little bit of grass and a few young trees and the sky. And that was it.

LL: The prisoners weren't allowed to play baseball and other sports?

DB: There was room enough for a softball field and

three handball courts and a couple of bocce courts and a basketball court, and that was the extent of it. It wasn't much for 750 men. We had one peculiar institution: three times during the summer, on Decoration Day, the Fourth of July and Labor Day, there was a prison "picnic." This was an all-day holiday on which there was outdoor cooking and eating and various sports contests. But it was a peculiar experience for an inmate for several reasons.

First of all, the idea of a picnic, in our culture, is always associated with bodily freedom and a choice of landscapes and places to escape to, especially for urban people, and the presence of children and families. So to transfer this tradition to the prison scene was boggling, to say the least. I think most prisoners found these days almost as hard to bear as Christmas or family birthdays or anniversaries, because what was meant to be a mitigation of the prison routine became instead another twist of the knife for many, a new way of realizing one's separation and powerlessness and sorrow.

Anybody could identify such holidays as prison days because you lined up as usual for food and drink and then peeled off in groups to eat with your friends on the grass. Then there were the games and the rewards. Of course money was not allowed, so the winners usually got a certain quantity of cigarettes, which were common currency. There were ball games and bocce games and even bridge tournaments and dominoes and chess and relay races and dashes. One picnic came off in foul weather. It had teemed rain all day long, yet the authorities wouldn't consent to transfer the picnic to the nearest sunny day. For reasons unknown to us, it had to be held on schedule. So the eating and racing proceeded in the rain, and I can remember the amazing sight of these people dashing around in the mud. It made the games seem a little more senseless even than they would have ordinarily. One of the dashes ended up against the far wall of the jail. This meant that people crossing the finish line had to stop very quickly, which was impossible in that weather. So two of the men were injured crashing into the wall.

LL: What kind of jobs did you and Philip have?

DB: Philip was assigned to the education department from the beginning. He never changed his job, mainly because it was a sinecure—he had nothing to do. The title of his job was something like "education clerk," which meant any number of things. Depending upon the number of clerks that were assigned there at a given time, one would answer the phone and keep the files and clean the classrooms, or there would be nothing to do.

Phil sedulously cultivated the art of disappearance. He would be found at almost any hour of the day in one of the back cubicles of the language lab, studying, writing letters, reading, or talking with prisoners. It was a very beautiful and fruitful existence—he got by with doing nothing for the prison and everything for the inmates.

I was assigned to the dental clinic in August of '70. My job was very difficult, both physically and emotionally. And yet I stuck with it because it was an important place to be, especially because it granted me access to the hospital and also to a number of prisoners who were in pain and needed a little compassion or friendship at that point. I spent practically a year up there.

LL: What were your duties?

DB: I was a so-called dental assistant; I did a variety of things like taking X-rays and mounting them and cleaning instruments and helping out at the chair, handing instruments or handling the paraphernalia for extractions and cleaning up afterward, and in general being available to the two professionals there.

LL: Isn't that the kind of job for which one is supposed to have had some training?

DB: I guess I got the training on the spot. I started gradually and, really, I found it of great interest. There was a dental lab connected with the place where we made plates for prisoners and took impressions. It was a good complete service for the men, especially for the poorer prisoners, some of whom had had no access to this quality of dental care for years and years. We did a lot of work for people who never would have gotten it outside. And that was a great satisfaction for me. Then, too, I always knew who was in the hospital. I knew also who was in trouble in the hospital, who was in the strip cell there, and I found ways of getting cigarettes and messages to them and in general informing outsiders as to the fate of sick prisoners. I just tried to be a mediator between official policy and the suffering that came down on people.

LL: After your attack, were you reassigned?

DB: No, I was reassigned because I applied for it. I think I could have kept my job in the clinic, but it would have been absolutely impossible for me physically to take the work up again. So I got a transfer to the education department also. I worked in the library for the last six months, until my parole. Up there, I helped people find books, talked to them, and in general kept a sense of the rhythms of the whole place, because everybody wandered in there by night or by day to find out what was going on. It was one of the few places where a prisoner could be during the day or evening where he wouldn't be challenged or thrown out.

LL: Did you do a lot of reading yourself?

DB: I always got a lot of reading done. Not so much at work, because there I was usually busy in a kind of off-hand, unofficial way. But I always had time in my cell for reading—in the late afternoons or evenings.

LL: Did you write any poems?

DB: A few poems. It was very nice to send poems out to people, and a relief to myself also. I was also interested in jiving up the awful prison paper that we were given to write letters on. In the education department I came on some unlined typing paper. Then I carved blocks out of nickel erasers and got hold of a set of watercolors, so that I was able to print designs on the letters I sent out. These were successful to a degree. At least they expressed my feeling that I was free even though in prison. I wanted, through some color and line and words and poetry, to say so to other people—people who were depressed because I was in jail.

3

LEE LOCKWOOD: What was the make-up of the prisoner population at Danbury? What proportion were embezzlers and crooks, what proportion were on drug charges, and what proportion were resisters?

DANIEL BERRIGAN: Well, the resisters were a small nucleus at any point, never more than a dozen or fifteen. There was a large, intensive and expensive federal drug program going on called NARA; they had the largest concentration of shrinks, social workers and other parasites around them.

LL: How many prisoners were in this program?

DB: About a hundred and fifty. But there were many more than that in prison for pushing, importing and using. I would say there must have been two hundred and fifty men in for some aspect of drugs. The rest would break down into various crimes against property. There were no "violent" people there, except the very few whose lives were being protected, who had been transferred there because they had been in danger in a high-security prison. But they were negligible and were never heard from. They were sort of hiding out there.

LL: So more than half of the prison were there for crimes against property?

DB: If you include the drug people, as I would, I would say that it was the whole prison.

LL: What kind of relations did you and Phil have with your fellow inmates?

DB: I would say that Phil and I must have known about five hundred of the men. We were undoubtedly the best-known people around. The prisoners were extremely friendly to us, in general. Their attitude ranged from simple curiosity to hard-core interest and a desire to really get in and talk. Of course, that led to a bid to come to our classes, where we could really go at things with them.

We had no difficulty at all on a simple social level. The difficulty came when we really began to talk about human change, social change, the society as such, rehabilitation, what it might mean to be a man in prison as a way of preparing to be a man outside, the break in continuity between the kind of life one had been leading and the kind of life one might come to lead. All these were very hard, close-up questions that we tried to raise, but they were very threatening to the majority. But—where aren't they?

LL: I'd imagine that it was naturally easier for Phil to make friends with other men, given his outgoing disposition, than it was for you.

DB: Phil's aptitude for creating a community around him and for "connecting" with prisoners, for taking them as they are and undergoing the endless disappointments of discovering the cracks in broken men, was beyond description. And it didn't begin in jail; his gift just became more and more apparent in a place like Danbury, because the wounds of human beings are more generally hidden outside than in.

I want to be very concrete about this. We must have been there at least four months before either of us was able to get with three or four people who would meet regularly to discuss anything. Not even heavy topics, but just our lives, or something that we were reading, or something we had discovered—*anything*. To sit down with people and try to engage them in serious conversation once or twice a week, that effort was almost too much. But Phil simply doesn't give up on things like this. And it's not merely that he wouldn't give up. He could retain, for whomever he met next, the same kind of hope that he'd had for the last guy who happened to disappoint him. He never approached the next guy with disappointment on his face.

LL: One senses that there is a special bond between you and Philip that goes far beyond the natural closeness of brothers, something unique and remarkable. Do you feel that way about it?

DB: I suppose it's something that we've always taken for granted because it's always been there, but that doesn't make it any less a gift. I find it very hard to separate Phil's fate from mine, as a matter of affection and existence itself. I wouldn't know where his life began and mine ended. And I think either one of us would confess that if it weren't for the other, his own life couldn't go as well or as far. It's like Yeats's line about "doubling the heart's might"; the presence of a love, a very deep love, enlarges one's strength and enables one to go a great deal further. That is certainly true with us, and it's part of our grief, too.

I was thinking, the night after I left prison, it seems as though in these last years I have had, again and again, the experience of leaving Phil in jail and going out. It had only happened once before, but it seemed as though it had happened many times because I could never forget it: the awful moment of saying good-by to him, knowing he was there and would be there, maybe for a long time.

On the other hand, my consolation is in his strength, his ability to cope and to infuse vitality into others. That, and the deep rightness of what he's into, as a matter of life and death. He would be the very first to score me for dwelling on the past or on his suffering. And I don't mean to do that anyway.

LL: You said earlier that you and Phil complement one another.

DB: Very much so. We're extremely different, and the difference became really up-close when we were thrown in jail together at Danbury. We came to realize how differently our lives had branched out in the previous two years, during which we had seldom met and had so little chance to dig into our lives together. That was one of the greatest gifts that the government could have given us, to toss us in there together, because each of us had to go back to the roots and find his beginnings again. We really talked things out in a way we hadn't done in a long time. So much had happened to him that I had been away from and that I had to be helped to understand. And that wasn't just since we went underground; it began way back before Catonsville.

) 65 (

LL: In what ways do you think you are complementary?

DB: I couldn't think of two more unlike people. But where we meet is in the discipline of nonviolence and the fact that we've known how to get along with very different people, how to enlist friendship in people different from ourselves. So when we two meet, the differences are, I think, enriching rather than abrasive. He might agree—it's too bad he isn't here to talk about this—that I tend to work much more out of the imagination than he does. His development has been, in a very rigorous way, political. His reading, his writing, everything he does is in that direction, and his experience with the art forms is rather passive. I mean, he appreciates very good things, beautiful things; but I don't think he feels that he ought to help make them.

LL: Would you say that you're more metaphorical than Philip?

DB: Oh, yes, much more. And more roundabout, and serpentine. More Jesuitical. (Laughs)

For instance, our attitudes toward and dealings with prisoners were very different. I tended to freewheel, while he tended to feel responsible for the formation of study and discussion groups. I did that too, but not with the same intensity or to the same degree. For instance, I couldn't stand always lining up in the chow hall with the same people.

LL: You were supposed to do that?

DB: No, you did what you wanted. But Phil's friends wanted to be around him and eat with him and he wanted to be with them. I tended to go and get my tray and sit with anybody. These are more tendencies than anything hard and fast, but that was one example. I just couldn't stand being with the same people all the time, while he felt that it was good, because it got into very deep stuff. But we both were involved with people in our houses, mainly studying the gospels, and we both were in the great books class. We were agreed on the value of all that. And of course, his impact on the community at large was very great.

LL: Did you find any receptivity at all among your fellow inmates to your ideas about the Vietnam War and about resistance? Could you talk to them about these things?

DB: We weren't supposed to, but we did. We did our very best at it, though I would say it was tough from every point of view. Life in prison is so wearing on young people; the winter settles in, and people seem to hibernate and hide out. Then too, most young people are involved in very precarious human relationships with those outside; family situations are rough, marriage, difficulties of all kinds. In a sense, by opening up these subjects, you were adding another burden to their condition, and most of them really couldn't bear it. I think we came to realize with ever more compassion that a man's life must be reasonably well glued together before he can begin to move in on the horrors of public life and of society.

LL: If so, that rules out at least ninety percent of all of us.

DB: Maybe. But what we found ourselves doing most of the time at Danbury was just shoring people up from day to day, being courteous and cheerful over the long haul. We tried to show an interest in their lives and families, and then tried to find the few who might go a little bit further.

LL: In *Night Flight To Hanoi*, which is my favorite among all your books of prose, you used the metaphor of "prison" in a paradoxical sense. You described how you were flying to Hanoi with Howard Zinn to accept release from the North Vietnamese of the first three American prisoners of war. And you asked yourself whether you were really liberating those men, or whether you were not in fact bringing them back to another kind of prison, a spiritual prison from which they had been able to escape only by being shot down over North Vietnam and confronted with the impact of their deeds, and thereby with the need to question their own lives and values, which might be the first step toward any true moral liberation. Is that a fair paraphrase of your idea?

DB: Okay—right.

LL: I wonder then whether you found that this paradox had any application to the condition of prisoners at Danbury? Was jail in any sense a "liberating" experience for any of them—or for you and Philip, for that matter?

DB: Phil and I both struggled hard to relieve the Dead Sea level of existence at Danbury. Not just for ourselves, because we could make it ourselves. But we tried to do something for others, and that was really a monumental job. We struggled with education and tried to get books in and initiated a suit against the government on the question of First Amendment rights, all of this with a view to helping change happen faster. Because even then we had a sense that the ground was quaking under our feet, that the prison scene was changing very rapidly. It became a question of how many people could be salvaged in the meantime, because we couldn't go by *their* timetable, which would have been slowly to mitigate a few things and slowly to grant a few favors. But the application of human rights was our point—rights that were being violated at every moment—and the dehumanization which was the daily portion of the prisoners.

To get to your question, I think we were too involved in trying to get a few practical things started to be able to reflect on the whole situation at the time. Prison was interesting because we made it interesting; it was difficult because we made it difficult. And we continually risked longer sentences and further indictments and denial of parole because we believed that this scene was just as truly our responsibility as, say, the underground was, or as Catonsville was. Prison is where we were, and these were the men we were among.

If there's anything that struck me with regard to the difficulties, it had to do not with the impermeable wooden face of things around us but with the human wreckage of the prisoners themselves, especially the young people. And the very small number, hardly a handful, that one could count on for anything when the chips were down, or who could sustain any sort of moral or psychic continuity so that they could stay with something and build on it. It was very rare, very rare. Most of them were wrecked before they got here by the lives they had led, by the relationships they had broken by coming to prison, and then by the obsession to get out. So the possibility of raising questions of fundamental liberation was very dim.

LL: Was it your experience that prison is primarily punitive rather than rehabilitative in nature?

DB: I recall that once a group of us were talking about the allocation of funds in a typical prison. Eighty-five to ninety percent of the government funds at Danbury go to purely custodial, law-and-order-keeping tasks and salaries, and a mere five to ten percent is devoted to health, education and welfare. It's a great deal like the National Budget; the priorities that operate in society at large are very strongly reflected there, up-close.

The stalemate and ruin that are wrought on people outside are a little more diffuse, because outside most can move at least a bit on their own. But in prison things were very up-close. You saw on every hand at Danbury the gap between society's rhetoric and its performance, between real values and stated values. They had guards stumbling all over one another whose days were marked by idleness and inertia and intellectual stagnation. They didn't even require a high school diploma for guards, because the job is such a dead end that no one with a chance for something better would want it. And the salaries are very low.

It was the same with the other employees. It was almost impossible to find a real person on the premises, someone who would level with you, someone who would risk anything for the welfare of the men, someone with the imagination to initiate or encourage a new direction. The scene in the mornings there ought to be filmed some day, the moment when the prisoners leave for their jobs and the outside employees enter and cross the compound. I don't know how many there are—maybe fifty or sixty of them—lugging their little brief-cases, to face another day. You can read on those faces the denial of hope and of value and of joy. You find no response when you look at them; none of them greet you, none of them pretend that they regard you as a human being. I had a kind of childish expectation at the beginning that they would find Phil and me interesting, that maybe one of the psychiatrists or doctors or social workers or teachers would want to talk to us. But that never happened, or else it happened so superficially that it made no difference.

LL: You see prison as a microcosm of the society at large. I remember that in your letter to Judge Roselle

Thomsen, the judge at the Catonsville trial, you spoke of the impossibility of rehabilitation in prison without fundamental change in the whole society.

DB: It seems to me that short of that understanding, we're simply turning out good robots who, after prison, reenter the same old scene, the same old values. That's really all there is to it. And in prison, the very conception of the word "rehabilitation" is corrupted by circumstances that don't allow human beings to emerge.

Maybe I could speak of two or three steps that I would see as necessary before there can be a new awareness and self-understanding on the part of prisoners.

In the first place, a renunciation of the economic values, which I think are very closely connected with the moral values, or the lack of same, that have brought men to prison. Most have been convicted of breaking the society's rules regarding its own good housekeeping. At Danbury, as I have said, they are in prison for nonviolent crimes: that is, because they have violated property rights in some way or other. Which is to say that they haven't seriously challenged the rules of the society. They've broken the rules, but they've played the game, and that's the way they have defined their lives thus far: by either keeping or breaking the rules of the consumer game.

These are "sins" against money, but they are unconscious sins, in the sense that they are not protests against the sins of the economy itself, the sins of a money society. The prisoners have paid deep and real tribute to Caesar by breaking his rules and taking the punishment involved, without ever really questioning why those rules exist in the first place or how they might have challenged them or questioned them or ignored them.

I would think this is the first step: to develop a consciousness that would help them to see that the game whose rules they were breaking is not worth playing in any case. To help them see that, for the majority of people, the game is not working very well; that it is really bringing about the alternation of hot and cold war that goes by the name of societal normalcy, God help us.

The second step would be some possibility of growth while men are in prison. And I connect that to what I spoke of earlier: intellectual and moral discipline, small groups, reading, content courses, good discussions and seizing opportunities for reflection, and so on.

One has to face the fact that most prisoners are childish—children of their culture. But the culture turns on them and, even in their punishment, continues the process of distraction and disintegration that brought them to prison. So that having time on their hands becomes a form of punishment instead of a form of release. They're inundated by a childish atmosphere of cheap reading, television, the commissary, all that kid stuff. The whole scene keeps their lives childish as a way of avoiding consciousness. Obviously, the government doesn't want anything else to happen. The government sets the atmosphere, sets the priorities, sets the use of money and of men just to keep that game going.

The third step would be, I think, the return to society of men who have passed from prisoner to resister.

LL: "Resister" in what sense?

DB: Resister in a sense which he has discovered himself in the light of his past, in the light of his family, in the light of his talents. Such a man would be ready, in some significant and serious way, to say "No" to the values that he had formerly embraced, and to live in a new way, with new consciousness.

LL: What are the fundamental things which you see as being wrong with our society? You speak of the need for men to become "resisters." Resisters of what?

DB: The simplest and most concrete way I could put it is to say that the society is hellbent on war and death as its normal regimen. The resources of society are more and more turned in that direction, by either military or paramilitary means. Death is the chief function and tool of preventing moral change and growth. And in order to say "No" to that kind of hellbent death project, one has to be ready to take resistance seriously, simply because one has grown to the point where he's taking life seriously.

The death obsession of our society—we could spend a couple of volumes on that. But I point to Vietnam, to our wasteful, long-lasting, insane pursuit of death there, with no political or human justification; our inability to withdraw and repent and begin to live in a civilized fashion. This war from one point of view can be called symptomatic; from another, it points very directly, it seems to me, to the death wish, the death urge that is now at large, that more and more deeply permeates our institutions and procedures. By way of example one thinks of the recent revelations of the army's computerizing of citizens' lives. It's a way of ensuring that the death game go on, and that those who resist it be known and punished.

LL: What is the correlation in your view between the "death urge" of American society and your vision of our society as being consumer-oriented?

DB: You know, living in the midst of men who were being punished for being bad consumers was a very interesting experience. As I said earlier, they were not being punished because they wouldn't consume. They were being punished because they consumed according to rules that weren't good for the game, or because they wanted to consume more than their share, or because they wanted to seize and consume too quickly. Deep in their minds was the idea that the good American, the good human being, is simply the good consumer. And most of them will return to that game untouched by any urge to change.

It seems to me that a society such as this, bent on consuming and on producing for more consumption, ultimately ends up by consuming lives. It is for this reason that I see war as the inevitable other end of the consumer process. In order to justify and protect the game and allow it to expand into new areas of technology, war is inevitable. Because other people stand in the way, other people challenge us with other visions of reality, other ways of arranging human life, and this cannot be borne by the masters. So the death count, the body count, becomes the other end of the money count.

LL: Willard Galen, a psychiatrist, has done a lot of work in prisons, and he has written a book about resisters called *In The Service of Their Country*. In it he states that he found it universally true that prisoners who go into prison as pacifists become converted by the prison system to the necessity of violence and lose their pacifism. And David Miller, who was once a student of yours, has recently coauthored another book with Howard Levy, *Going to Jail*, in which he testifies personally to a similar transformation. He says he has renounced both his Catholicism and his pacifism as a result of his prison experience. Did you find that the same thing happened among the resisting community at Danbury?

DB: I'd like to step back a bit and say how struck I was recently by the statement of James Douglas, the young professor in Hawaii who poured blood on the secret files of the Air War Command there. He invoked in his action the earliest of the blood-pouring incidents, for which Philip is still in jail—that in Baltimore in 1963. That's a nine-year continuum which I find intriguing— the idea that both Catholicism and nonviolence are still very much alive and heard from, through all the copouts and losses and deaths and jailings and official insanities of the intervening years. On the one hand, a fast turnover and disposability of human beings in most phases of the movement. On the other hand, a Catholic continuity. This recognition scene is constantly occurring, with its familiar leitmotif of respect for life and disrespect for the pretensions of property. I bring it up because I believe we have here a kind of spiritual current for a discussion of this kind.

The early sixties were marked by the jailing of that generation of pacifists who came mainly out of the Catholic Worker background. David Miller is a luminous example of such a man. He came out of service to the poor to a profound understanding of the war in its destructive and antihumane elements. His consciousness began in college, certainly, but the actual experience of life among the poor I think sharpened the edge of his understanding to the point where he was ready for jail as the war hottened up.

What David and others found in jail is another matter entirely. I can reconstruct it from Phil's experience with them, say from 1964 onward, when he and David were together at Allenwood and I was visiting them there frequently. We both realized that something negative and regrettable was taking place in that early community of resisters. They seemed unable to retain or develop within prison the reasons that had brought them there, or to find in one another the moral solidarity required to survive the onslaught of prison authority, which is, of course, a vicious and disintegrating force.

So they tended to peel off and do their sports thing and their reading. They certainly were mentally alive, but they were wounded, and they lost, by the attrition of the months, the force of a common bond, a common rationale, a common vision of the future, as I would judge. As a result, practically all of those I know who came out of prison, including David Miller, declared themselves very different, and indeed were very different, from the young men who had gone in. One mark of this change was their great difficulty in getting their marriages and families going again. In most cases, there was a simple breakup very shortly after their release.

Another mark, of course, was their attitude toward the Church and indeed toward faith in general. Still another, as you've already hinted, and as Galen and David Miller both bring out, was their attitude toward nonviolence. And that maybe is the deepest and most regrettable way of putting the changes that occurred. The prison system, and thereby the military, had in a real sense won out. Because nonviolent men had been converted, by the violence inflicted upon them, to violence as method and as ethos.

LL: Here is what Dr. Galen says on that subject.

"The clearest manifestation of the rising hostility that the prisons generate in what has been essentially a non-hostile population is in the almost unanimous conversion from the concept of non-violence. I realize that the conversion from non-violence to violence is a process that is going on among the young in or out of the prisons, but the switch seems particularly dramatic with the imprisoned group because of the intensity of their original dedication to non-violent positions."

What was different, if indeed there was a difference, about your experience with resisters at Danbury?

DB: First of all, I should say that strong reservations about Galen's book were later expressed by those who had been interviewed. So I would go a little easy on so definite a statement as the one you quote. I believe there was a marked difference between what he describes and what the men later claimed to have said to him.

But could I begin with a couple of convictions that Phil and I entered prison armed—or disarmed—with? First of all, we were not convinced that to have come to jail with high ideals was any guarantee that these ideals would be automatically retained or would be socially available within the prison. Secondly, we realized that most resisters wrongly supposed that a community of conscience in jail would be an easy or a natural thing, that men would come together easily because they had come to jail in resistance to the war. Neither of these things, it seemed to us, was true in fact. Community in prison would be a difficult and even an abrasive task. Community had to be worked at. The reason that brought one there had to be consistently shared and reviewed. Otherwise, men just ricocheted off each other. As new men came, they either found a community that was struggling with these questions and with its own identity and future, or else they found nothing and became part of a generally characterless, disenchanted, bitter population.

We believed that community was possible. We believed that it had to be worked at *anywhere* in one's life, and we set to work at it in prison. And I think out of that came actual events which showed that something different was in the air at Danbury. The first was the fast of June of 1971; the second was the general strike, the nonviolent work strike, that broke out shortly after my release; the third was the vigil against the war by prisoners who climbed the water tower in April of 1972.

LL: As I remember you telling me, the nuclear seed of those actions was a "great books" discussion class that you and Phil led as a kind of extracurricular activity sanctioned by the prison. How was that formed?

DB: That was a three-month struggle. The authorities were of course very distrustful of anything that we would have part in on a sanctioned basis. So it wasn't until late November of 1970 that we finally got the clearance to go ahead. Our idea was very simple. We were anxious to come together not on their terms but our own, to try to survive week by week, under scrutiny and with snitches in the class. We didn't want to come together on the basis of these half-witted Skinner or Esalen sensitivity sessions that had become so current in the prison and that were getting nowhere—as the inmates themselves would testify. Therefore, we always insisted that the priority in class belonged to ideas, ideas that came to us from outside our experience and that would have to ricochet off it, be integrated or rejected, so that our experience would get some light on it and we wouldn't be simply chasing our own entrails and calling it living.

This was a continuous struggle. The turnover was great; a lot of younger people disliked the discipline of books. I think that attitude came out of the sixties, especially the SDS experience. Perhaps also as a matter of self-protection or egoism, they wanted to declare their independence of this or that thinker, this or that writer, on the assumption that their own experience was rich enough to sustain itself. But we did our best to combat that attitude, to make whatever discussion came up work with and compare itself with and contrast itself against the particular book that we were discussing, so that we would never degenerate into an ingroup that got nowhere.

We started with St. Matthew's Gospel, which we studied thoroughly for a couple of months, at least some of the key passages. By that time, it had become clear that if the class was to survive the winter—practically none of these efforts ever did—it was going to have to belong to the members; there could be no lectures or dependences upon Phil and myself as gurus. Yet, at the same time, in a subtle and indirect way, we had to be there challenging them, because, at least at that stage of things, the class couldn't survive without us. So we were determined that we would take it seriously and would always be present, even if it went down to three or four or five members, as it frequently did that winter.

Toward the spring, though, it began to pick up, and all through the spring and summer and autumn it varied from about a dozen to twenty or twenty-five. Anything over a dozen became unwieldy and as difficult as three or four. But miraculously the class went on for the sixteen remaining months of my time there. And it's *still* going. I would think, modestly and concretely, it was the best single leaven for the pervasive influence that these young people began to have in their living-quarters. And that resulted, I think, from the change in attitude this discipline induced, week after week, and the relationships and conversations and attitudes that arose between themselves and other prisoners.

LL: What books did you read in the class?

DB: Two basic works on nonviolence: Gandhi's autobiography and Erikson's *Gandhi's Truth.* We also read *Gulliver's Travels,* Locke's *On Human Liberty,* your own book on *Castro's Cuba,* an anthology called *Sisterhood Is Powerful, Basic Works of Marxism,* Philip Slater's *On American Culture* and Lifton's *Death in Life,* plus others.

I think the criterion by which we chose our books was a very interesting one. A vote was always taken before a book was picked. Sometimes we found that we had made a mistake, that the book really wasn't working for us. For instance, we simply couldn't stay with the thousand pages of *Basic Works of Marxism.* After about three weeks of trying, it was evident that we had to choose certain sections or drop the book entirely. So we decided to drop it; perhaps they'll come back to it later.

There was practically no book that met the expectations of everybody in the class, and that was a continuing hassle also. Some people had too much background, some had too little to be able to approach a book as an experience that would yield fruit if one stayed with it. So all sorts of anguished cries arose in the course of each book. But the majority vote carried in most cases. Even when the readers were most critical, there were very valuable criticisms offered. We often wished, in fact, that the authors could have been present to deal with our questions firsthand. I think they would have gained a great deal.

The severest critiques, by the way, came to rest on

some of the most prestigious authors. In general the gripes reflected the bias of young people against even the most enlightened psychiatric methods and religious insights. I found that linkage very interesting. For instance, most young prisoners could not abide Eric Erikson. Most of them also thought Lifton's book on Hiroshima was a cultural and human invasion of the Japanese people, that he might better have spent his time—I remember this judgment coming up frequently —looking at the other end of the spectrum, interviewing the power boys who had brought such devastation to the Japanese, finding out what was sick about our President and military that they could have brought the bomb down. I found this very just within limits— and I would tend to be very broad on my limits.

LL: I guess you're saying that the prisoners were as interested in where the authors stood as in the problems that they were dealing with; whether they were biographers or historians or psychiatrists, merely describing and analyzing things wasn't enough for your students —they wanted to know where the authors stood and why?

DB: Yes. Actually I think this would shed light on their criticism of Galen's book also. They felt that in this book and books like it, they were being morally strip searched, strip mined, and that this defined the rottenness of the American scientific method. That is to say, you bring home to the museum examples of the destruction or death that you yourself have dumped on other people. And it was never clear to the prisoners why there had to be this moral gap between methods of inquiry and ethical consciousness.

To take an example that I think is to the point, their criticism of Gandhi's *Autobiography* was different in kind from their criticism of Erikson's discussion of Gandhi's self-revelation, but there never was the remotest question about the quality or the meaning of the man. Whereas in Erikson's case, they said, "Well, where's *he* been all his life?"

This was even true, in a parallel way, of some of their difficulties with the Church versus the life of Jesus, you know? They had absolutely no quarrel with the substantials of Jesus' life and death in its nonviolent character, in its self-understanding as gift to history, gift to community, all that. But, at the same time, they expressed a revulsion against churchmen and their claims upon the lives of others.

LL: Which books were the most successful?

DB: Of course, success is a difficult thing to measure in prison. The books that stimulated people in the most positive way and made them most long to learn more were your Cuba book, the Sisterhood book and Slater's book. And, of course, *Gulliver's Travels* turned into a marvelous fiesta, an inspired freak show. Gandhi's autobiography, in a totally different way, was almost a gospel; almost, you would say, an inspired book, a gift.

But let me say something more about the Sisterhood book. All of us felt that in undertaking a book like that, a group of men discussing women's liberation, we were acting like the liberal whites of the early sixties who used to gather to talk about "those Negroes." So we finally got the prison to agree that two young women who taught classes there could sit with us for a couple of hours one afternoon. They couldn't stay on for evening sessions because "they might get raped"—quote, unquote. But they could take their class time and sit with us after having read the book.

One was black and the other was a white woman

who was just back from Chile and was teaching English to the Spanish-speaking in the prison. I would say that both of them learned a great deal in reading the book, but that neither of them was any help to us. Mainly because they didn't know us. We weren't in any of the basic classes that they were teaching, and they found it very difficult to connect, first of all, with the boiling consciousness of the book itself—it really puckered their eyebrows that women were thinking this way about women—and then to connect with us through the book.

It turned into a minor disaster, and we got nowhere. But what *did* get somewhere was interesting. On a certain night in the middle of the class one of the young resisters suggested that for any honest discussion it was important to open up about the women in the lives of the class members. Why couldn't we start by talking about those women, those occasions, those experiences in or out of marriage that had meant a great deal or had been destructive in our own lives? That really started something. I think it was the only substitute we could have for the actual presence of women who could have met those issues. The discussion initiated that night went on for two more sessions in a round robin, and it helped everyone. Because the book had struck hard, it had struck low and hard at everyone in there. I mean everyone. It was almost like picking up your first passionate book about blacks and realizing what a great area of life had been hidden from your conscience. It was interesting also that that book helped us understand the connection between the crimes that brought men to Danbury and their relationships to women in general.

The influence of the book went beyond just the members of the group itself. Other prisoners were always dropping in and out of the class. Occasionally, if they found a book that piqued their curiosity, they would stay for a while. In this case, some of them found themselves confronted with a book that implied that exploitative attitudes toward money and drugs and possessions of all kinds inevitably led to the exploitation of women. And I used to put it as crudely as I could to them, just to excite anger and response from these people. My statement was that behind every crook there was an exploited woman. Such a thesis, of course, had very interesting consequences, and it had the element of truth required to bring a larger area of truth into view. One could in any case see from the women who visited the prison, from their self-understanding, the way they dressed and the way they conducted themselves, whether or not they were an extension of the man they were visiting, another possession, or whether they were individuals endowed with a dignity and a sense of themselves. And it was extremely rare to find an inmate who had any sense of women that went beyond his sense of his car or his bankroll or his machismo.

We were infected by that too, people like Phil and myself, in a different way; we also needed to plow up these attitudes and to face this rising tide of women's consciousness. It was too easy for resisters to declare that they were pure in this regard because they were pure in other regards; for example, in their attitudes toward generalized public violence. I think the outcome of the reading of *Sisterhood is Powerful* was that we came to understand how unconscious we had been of the cries of anguish and fury that rose from the text and were rising in the world around us. We had some work cut out for us, we realized.

LL: Did you encounter any antagonism among the students over the fact that you and Phil were priests and therefore not burdened with this kind of relationship, any accusation that you were perhaps speaking out of turn?

DB: Well, the fact that we were not burdened with *this* sort of relationship didn't mean that we didn't have other kinds of burdens about women and ourselves. And we didn't make any great thing about the fact of celibacy. I think it was part of their general acceptance of us. They were able to understand that celibacy had given us a certain liberty in our decision to come to jail, and also that there were other ways of relating to women than theirs. And we spoke very freely of that, of our deep friendship with women over the years.

But I think we also had to confess that we hadn't been as sensitive as we should have been to the legal, economic, family, religious, and specifically the Catholic exploitation of women as revealed in that book.

The atmosphere of that class ranged from the deeply discouraging to what Sam Melville would have called the "ecstatic." On reflection, I think I understand his mysterious statement, in one of his letters, that "Revolution is ecstasy." I could discern that—the profound, incandescent, spiritual change that was occurring in such a heartbreaking way in the young faces around me. The sight induced in me a sense of them and of myself that was too deep for tears and certainly too deep for words. And I understood at certain points, at very brief moments during that class, what the Greeks meant by ecstasy, the "standing outside oneself" in an atmosphere of joy and fulfillment and inclusion of other lives. One can believe afterward that he has attained a leap in his very life, in his very existence, that he has forged new bonds with the lives of others which go beyond anything rational or predictable.

I had felt this now and again in my life in a classroom experience. But to have it occur in jail was something altogether special, because I have always looked upon these young resisters as the key to whatever future we have: that is to say, people who in decent times would have been stepping into high public office and professional life. There they were, the men of our own history, mythologized in our own revolution and in revolutions around the world. It was quite clear to me that they would end up either dead or in charge of the future, and that we were helping prepare them for either eventuality. And that was very good.

LL: It's certainly a remarkable thing to have happen inside a prison, and probably the only really rehabilitative kind of experience that any of those people had, judging from the description of the general tenor of prison life you gave earlier.

DB: I think it was. The difference between the mentality that was being forged in the class and the general mentality of the prison used to come home to me at times when there would be an outside lecture open to the whole prison. On such occasions, there might be forty or fifty prisoners together. Members of our class would usually be silent on these occasions, I think first of all trying to give room to others and secondly trying to learn their thinking. But it was very sobering, as a discussion would emerge on some subject, to see that most of the prisoners were fantasizing about a future which was in no sense different from the life they had led before. One got the terrifying sense that the only thing sustaining them in prison was this dream on the horizon that they could take up again the lives of comfort and self-indulgence and distraction which they had known outside and which had been both the culture's gift to them and the culture's revenge upon them. They hadn't come in any sense to the self-understanding that would enable them to say first of all, in the coldest historical sense, that that past is quickly being destroyed, being declared impossible, and secondly, that it isn't worth a damn anyway.

I would say this was true especially of the wealthy crooks, who were still wedded to America, who still looked upon themselves as deviants from the Dream, and whose persistent illusion was that they could go back to it; that since they had buried their cache at the end of the rainbow, it would still be there untarnished, winking at them. It was very sad, really. It was part of the dislocation of their lives, of the fact that they had so little to cling to; it was their attempt to cushion the dreadful alienation of being in prison.

LL: Did any of those "crooks" find their way into your class, or was it made up only of resisters?

DB: Practically none of them could stand the atmosphere of the class for more than one try. They came and went; they came out of curiosity because they had heard about us, and they sat in various states of bewilderment and then were never seen again. It was just too hot.

LL: Some of them must have been pretty intelligent and even well-educated.

DB: They were extremely intelligent, but I don't think it is unfair to say that, in general, they were too old and too fixated around the only events that had meant anything to them in their lives. When they wanted to talk about their lives, very little had happened since the Second World War. Those were their moments of glory. It was as though they were playing their own Patton scenario. That, and the family and money and the pervasive, sour sense of the injustices wrought upon them in prison—this was pretty much the substance of their lives. Most of them hadn't read a book in years.

It was a strange thing to reflect at times that they were of my generation, and I had come up through at least roughly the same events. And yet, Phil and I sat there listening to the next generation to find out what was going to happen and to help it happen, while the prisoners our age were absolutely bewildered—except for those very few who at least respected their own sons for taking a different turn.

LL: You were encouraging everybody who came into the class to reexamine the structure and fabric of their lives and to think about new ways of confronting the power structure. I would think that kind of thing would seem very threatening to men whose only thought was to get out of jail and back to their old lives as quickly as possible.

DB: Right. I think we were dealing with two different conceptions of that foul, misused and bedraggled word "rehabilitation," which was so often cast in our faces as a cover for atrocious and antihuman official activity. But in the case of the ordinary moneyed criminal, the acceptance of that word meant he accepted the transition from inmate to citizen, with all that implied; accepted the American scheme and dream, and himself as both sharer and partaker of it. On the other hand, the way we translated that word into our activity meant the spiritual rebirth of the prisoner, so that he would pass from an inmate to a resister, a resister indeed against the very society which had placed him there.

For those whose political decisions had brought them to prison, this was easily grasped. But the interesting fact was that, in the case of a certain number of younger prisoners, that rebirth actually occurred *in prison,* as indeed it had occurred earlier to people like Cleaver and Jackson and Melville. That was evident in the number of those who had been sent to prison for drugs or embezzling or auto theft who went to Harrisburg immediately after their release from Danbury to work on behalf of the defendants at the trial. And there will be more of them going from prison to other centers of social conflict in the future. Many of them will never return to their old ways of life.

LL: Judging from the list of books that were used in your class, you didn't deal with questions specifically relevant to blacks. Were there any blacks in your class? Was black awareness one of the themes that you took up?

DB: The blacks would come and go. Mainly, I judge, this was because they had put nothing together in their own community. The parallels between the blacks in prison and the whites in prison, at least at Danbury, were very striking, because the criminal offenses crossed over all the lines of white-and-black. We had one black resister who took a very active part in the strike in 1972. And I would say that when I left there, there might have been five blacks that would enter into activity that included whites. They would enter our class as they would enter a class on black history—because there was something valuable there. But the most articulate and understanding of the blacks at Danbury found their own situation in prison extremely discouraging simply because so much of the criminality was connected with the abuse of their own people through drugs and money crimes.

) 89 (

I would also say, in a way that I hope isn't excessively prideful, that they didn't have the equivalent of Phil and myself to help something get going, except toward the end, when this young black resister came in. He had been an actor and TV personality and had gotten five years in a Southern court for refusing induction. He had been turned in by his own father, who was the president of a college in Connecticut. So he came in like a Roman candle, with all his talents exploding around us. But his was the first serious attempt in the black community to put anything together worthy of attention.

LL: Do you think that blacks stayed away from the class because they didn't trust you and Phil, as whites, to deal meaningfully with the questions that were urgent to them?

DB: I suppose there was some of that feeling. But when such a thing was hinted at, I would ask, "What are you doing among yourselves?" And the answer was always, "Very little." There had been at least three attempts we knew of to get a black history course going, led by inmates or outsiders—both were available. But nothing got very far.

You see, I still have to explain to myself the chemistry of the change that brought about the strike shortly after I left Danbury. This obviously crossed all lines; something very deep was at work there that suddenly exploded, and I don't know quite how to explain it. I know it was connected with the presence of five key blacks who simply said, "We're going for broke, and you'd better follow." I think it's quite evident that something important happened at that point.

LL: So you think that it was the presence of yourself and Philip at Danbury which prevented the kind of

change that occurred in other prisons in the lives of resisters like David Miller who opted out of nonviolence
as a result of their prison experience? Is Dr. Galen
wrong in being categorical about the inevitability of
prison life provoking this change, this "conversion," as
he calls it, from nonviolence to violence?

DB: I'm struck by the implication of your question:
the utter failure of my generation to stand with anything, that Second World War generation that came
into positions of authority and of professional prestige
at the outbreak of the sixties and that had nothing to
contribute to the moral crisis of the younger people at
that time. Such people were, in effect, as the war developed, the Good Nazis in charge of whatever Nazifying
methods were expedient. And that's illustrated in the
prison scene, in the utter fatuousness and flabbiness of
the prisoners of my age, in their inability to understand
prison changes.

With practically no help from us, a new generation
had been asked to create itself whole cloth out of itself.
And this doesn't work very well, biologically or spiritually speaking. It seems to me that the creative factor
naturally in nature, and in grace as well, is always
the older generation who is capable of fostering life,
whether in the spirit or in the flesh. And when this older
generation is simply not there, the younger people don't
do too well among themselves. Frenzies, obsessions,
drug dreams arise; and practically the only ones of my
generation heard from are absurd, destructive people
like Dr. Leary. They get quoted and followed, and they
soon become the diabolical gurus that lead young people, at worst, into didactic violence and, at best, into
nirvana, into nowhere, into flatland.

I guess I'm coming to your question by saying that

it isn't that we were there at Danbury—that's not what strikes me—it's that *nobody* was anywhere else. On the Cornell campus during the sixties I could see what happened to young people who had no one of my generation around them—whether in the family, in the churches, on the professor's podium, in the shrink's office—no one whose lives could say, "Look—we still can offer something, and we invite you to follow; this is the direction and these are the tactics that brought us where we are; and to be where we are is humanly valuable." There's nobody who can talk that way. There are either theorists of religion or theorists of politics or theorists of this and that, but there are very few whose lives are planted where human life is in the breach. And I think this made the difference.

Speaking of Dr. Leary, I can remember vividly the impression made on all of us when he escaped from jail in California, landed in Algiers and issued that manifesto to the youth of America. I recall the fury with which Phil and I read that letter in prison. We found it food for worms, we found it food for illusion and bankruptcy and death, and we said so. It took some time for our conviction to be verified, because people were seduced by the fact that Leary had been made a victim by the society and given an outrageous sentence. All of this was true. But the deepest thing he was conveying in the letter, the thing they were buying whole cloth, was: Number one, drugs lead somewhere; Number two, violence leads somewhere; and Number three, if you can pull a caper like I did and escape from the law, you too can direct the future in the way I'm doing with this letter. And we found each of those pretensions morally and humanly outrageous.

It was a long, long struggle to convey that to the

large numbers of intelligent and sharp young people who were in our midst there. I don't think we succeeded in many cases. I think that there has been some mysterious juncture between the American dream and the promise that the drug culture offers. And that combination induces a state of mind that is extremely difficult to penetrate. Because once you've stepped over the line and gotten into that kind of promised land, you become utterly indifferent to the fate of others.

LL: Could you be more explicit about what you mean by "the juncture between the American dream and the promise that the drug culture offers"?

DB: In the middle class at least, the American dream has said to successive generations: first, you can make it; and secondly, practically everybody under the flag is making it, at least in principle, at least in the Constitution, at least in the Bill of Rights, at least in the churches—in all those points where structures touch upon individuals. And the proof of two is one: *you're* making it, and therefore why shouldn't others? The drug culture offers a pervasive and persuasive proof of this. It is possible now to engineer instant happiness without the sweat and tears of social or individual change. It's possible to enter into instant conversion of heart toward nonviolence and toward personal beatitude. The acquisition of all attitudes necessary for the future is a matter of swallowing, sniffing, smoking. Therefore the dream is verified in the lives of drug people who have the space and time and background and money and clothing and music (and now the drugs) as paraphernalia of the dream, as engineering factors in the product. And lo, the dream is here.

Now, when the dream lands one in prison, that's not a serious disturbance of the dream because, after all,

Dr. Leary was in prison, and after all, Dr. Leary cut loose and issued this very important document to all of us. Granted the letter is faintly disturbing, but we've really been remotely attached to violence anyway, at least in principle, even though we have never had to verify it or wreak it upon others or been subjects of violence ourselves. So to have Dr. Leary say that it's *really* important to kill a pig for the sake of a high, for the sake of verifying your experience and all that, that's not seriously disturbing. Not that any of us will ever do it, but it's a good, titillating thing to have said by your pope.

The breakthrough from that seduction to the kind of responsibility, the kind of patient struggle that we were sponsoring, was extremely difficult, and only in a few cases did it get anywhere. But at least I would say that toward the last six months of 1971, the drug people were not talking as beatifically and as stupidly about Leary as they had been. I think some of them were landing on reality and that it had a very different feel under the feet than the cloud he had described.

LL: It seems to me that as a priest, and especially a Jesuit, you have advantages over other people that might prepare you for either underground or prison. First of all, you have well-developed inner resources that come from years of training, including a strong sense of discipline. Then, your faith gives you a far stronger confidence in your own salvation than what most other people have. Moreover, as a celibate you are spared the family problems and responsibilities with which most of the rest of us are afflicted.

DB: Right. Some of the things you mention are tremendous—I don't know what to call them—graces or gifts or benefits. But they also have price tags on them, in the sense that one's responsibilities toward others increase as he is freed from their burdens.

While I was at Danbury I was struck by an interview with Robert Jay Lifton that I read somewhere. It seems to me that he has looked death squarely in the face in that Hiroshima book. So I was very taken by his remarks on the omnipresence of death in the modern world and our longing for immortality. I don't share with him and with most people the breakup of the idea that man is immortal—even though the religious force of that idea has, I think, gotten terribly lost, perhaps mainly because religion itself has given up on being a vehicle of immortality.

But I would say that Phil and I are not afflicted in a gnawing sense with the reality of death as it ordinarily strikes and depresses and weighs upon all sorts of people, including our fellow prisoners. For us, jail was rather a scene of life than of death. You went into it with the idea that you were actually a presence; not another integer of death, but a presence that speaks of a certain life. And that could be, I think, very anonymous and quotidian. It was a matter of cheerfulness, of being able to ride with burdens better than most of the other men were able. And of making their burden perhaps a little less intolerable, to that degree. Perhaps— I hope so.

4

LEE LOCKWOOD: At one point in jail you almost died from an injection of Novocaine given you while you were having dental work done. What happened?

DANIEL BERRIGAN: Well, the opinion which they ventured in the hospital was "a massive allergic shock."

LL: How could that happen?

DB: The heart specialist said that it could happen to anyone. They hit the wrong artery or something. It was supposed to go into a vein near the tooth, but instead it went into an artery that took it right to the heart.

LL: So you had a kind of heart attack?

DB: No, it wasn't the heart; it was more the lungs and the respiratory system. Like, I went blue, icy, right away; stiff. I was *dying!* It was incredible. They were working on me for about an hour.

LL: Were you conscious at all?

DB: Oh, yes—I was in and out. It's really very difficult to describe. I knew everything that was going on. I could hear all the voices around me. I could read the expressions on the faces. I knew it was very bad. I could see my own hand, all purple and blue and stiff, and my feet. And then I called for Phil. And I knew *he* was there. And then I would sort of go out again.

It was like being on a high, like "going up." You know the old paintings? One just sort of hovered above everybody, you know? It wasn't particularly unpleasant, except that I was a little chagrined. I thought a dirty trick was being played on me. I hadn't been told the rules of the game, and suddenly they were being applied. I mean, to die from a shot of Novocaine is a very absurd thing when you think you should go out big.

LL: You really thought that you were giving up the ghost?

DB: Actually, I was working very hard at staying alive. Of course, they were giving me oxygen, and I was fighting; in fact, fighting too hard—they were trying to calm me. But my heart was going like a chicken for five hours, four times a beat, until they got it under control. And then, in the ambulance on the way to the hospital, I nearly went again.

LL: You mean, all of this took place in the prison?

DB: They couldn't ship me out in the beginning, because I wasn't breathing. So, before they could get me down to the cardiac room in the hospital, they had to work on me with oxygen. They injected me with adrenalin, and so on. This went on for about an hour. And I was watching this clock—that was the strangest part of it. It was a wall clock, right above me. And I was very conscious of time. Like, five minutes ago I was with it, and then I had lost five minutes. And I was sort of recording what it was to be in time and out of time—very strange! Really weird. And I said some prayers, you know.

LL: What kind of prayers?

DB: Well, prayers just sort of to stay with whatever it meant. Because I was expecting momentarily to be ushered into the presence of the Iceman.

I was getting tired toward the end. I don't know how much longer I could have gone on. It's terrifying to have to fight for every breath. In that condition, in spite of yourself, you begin to say to yourself after a while, "What's it all about?" And how sweet it was to wake up, hours later, and find that I could breathe again without any difficulty, to conspire with the universe. It seemed as if the whole universe was breathing in harmony with me. It was an indescribable feeling.

LL: How did the press get wind of your attack? Did some prison worker tip them off?

DB: Probably—I'm not sure. But when I was being wheeled out, someone told me later, the warden picked up the phone and it was the AP. I wasn't even out of the prison grounds yet. The warden couldn't think of what to say—because he didn't really know what was going on—so he said, and this was later quoted all over: "Father Berrigan has suffered a spell." And someday I'm going to ask him if it was he who laid it on me. (Chuckles)

But I had some fantastic epiphanies during the whole experience. For example, I remember that as I floated there in the cardiac room, in my "waterbed," I could see all these disembodied faces. There was a partition with a glass for observing the patients. And, strangely enough, I could tell who the people behind it were just from their faces, even when there was no other indication. I remember the pumpkin features of the hospital administrators—who looked like the kind of persons who would overcharge the dead—and a guard, always a guard, staring at me quizzically, as though I were off his radar.

The prison officials were unhappy that I was there and that they were being subjected to a lot of phone calls and other upsettings of their sterile regime. So they would just puff up there and look in. And they kept instructing the nurses and others about keeping outsiders away from me. Then there were people cleaning up the ward; they would just look in with very nice faces because, I think, they were interested. A lot of them were Catholics. And here's this priest . . . When they would come around to vacuum-clean and all, they were always talking to me with sympathy. Then there were the doctors. And the doctors looked sweetly puzzled! (Chuckles) As though this diagnosis was going to take at least ten minutes, and they only had eight. And they would consult with one another behind this glass —I didn't even have to read their lips—one of them was suggesting to the other that the TV screen which was monitoring me looked a little puzzling, but it was settling down, and, "He is cooking merrily now." They looked at the screen, heads to one side, musingly; and, "Don't you think this?" And then the other one would say, "Well, yes, but don't you think that?" And then they would come to a synthesis.

LL: And do what?

DB: And depart! Collecting their pay check on the way out, I suppose.

But I don't want to be unfair to the doctors, because they were really, I thought, harassed, unhappy men who strangely enough wanted desperately to talk. One of the hard things about being sick was the number of people who wanted to talk. And I had so little strength. But these doctors were typical refugees from New York. One of them had taught at Columbia Medical School for ten years, a very distinguished man. And the other two had had big private practices and all that. And they had gotten out from the burning city, but they weren't finding much up in Connecticut. And they expressed their longing to come up to the prison and talk things over, but none of them knew how to deal with bureaucracies, so they just stewed in their own juices and never did get to it.

But they're rich, and their brows are furrowed, and their medicine is hyperexpensive, and they know that they're floating away from the mainland on ice floes, and they don't know how to get back.

LL: They sound like the kind of people you were trying to reach while you were underground.

DB: You know, I have had this feeling about medicine for so long, and it's really just surfacing. The terrible conditions not only among the poor people—everyone's saying now, "Don't get sick in America" as they used to say, "Don't get sick in jail"—but among these doctors too! They're at this in-between stage; they're too established to seize the reins of change, they've made their pile, their kids are nudging them, and they have fewer and fewer connections any more.

One of the common elements, too, among those I met—I talked at length with three of them—is that the Catholics find very little in their own Church any more. This is amazing, but it's true of people my own age, middle-aged people. And the most distinguished of them, this M.D. from Columbia, was a deeply religious man, I thought, with no Church affiliation at all. Yet another mooring has come unfastened for them: they don't have religious security any more. And the people, God help them, whom they come to admire, even on the religious scene—people like me! I mean, that in itself is enough to send one screaming out of Westchester.

LL: (Laughing) It's your ecumenical approach, I'm sure, that makes you available to them.

DB: Well, it was a little whiff of the outside world. You began to realize that it's not so terrible to be in a place like prison as long as your being there has meaning to someone, and you hear of it now and then. Meeting the medicos was another index to me of how quickly things were fraying outside. How terrifying it was to see that the deepest human relationships aren't really counting or working for people.

And this condition invades every area of people's lives, not only their professions. We didn't get much into the family scene, but it was quite clear that part of the anguish is that their own sons can't talk to them. And that's awful. Because revenge has come down on the people who thought that their profession was going to be a sea wall against the floods.

LL: Did you have a priest with you during the crisis?

DB: Oh, they came running from all directions. Some poor guy came in just after I'd arrived there, and he wanted to do the whole thing over me. But I said, "Well, I've just seen my brother, thank you."

LL: Did Phil give you Extreme Unction?

DB: No, but I had Phil around—that was Extreme Unction. Those days, I didn't want any hands laid on me that I didn't know about. (Laughing) I mean, this guy might have been paid by some chancery to get in and finish me off, for all I knew.

But he was so undone that finally I asked him for a blessing to calm him down. So that he wouldn't feel so badly at having to go back, as it were, empty-handed.

So, he broke into a Latin blessing! At which I wasted a lot of breath laughing, because I couldn't help it. And he went back to the rectory and told everyone there that in his traumatic state—*his* traumatic state, not mine!—he had been in such turmoil that he'd given me the blessing in Latin.

LL: What was the blessing?

DB: I don't even remember. I'm not too good at Latin.

But that wasn't the only interesting visit I had. The next day, the Pallbearers' Association sent down its three charter members: the warden, the Catholic chaplain and my caseworker. Now, I don't win many rounds, but I won this one, because I was asleep. So they tiptoed out again after viewing the body. But can you imagine that—the three of them coming in together?

LL: That might have been enough to give you a relapse.

DB: You're not kidding.

Anyhow, I used to sit up most of the night, because I couldn't sleep. There was death all around me. I was in this cardiac unit for five days. And a few of those poor people decided to go under toward dawn, and it was a really shocking, noisy passage—for everybody. Not because death was there—that's fine—but because of the way these people were being treated. Somebody was very determined to keep them somehow respiring. If you can imagine breathing cabbages, that's about all they were. The hospital has a signal system, it's sup-

posed to be very advanced, very technologized—they
send out this panic button roar. All I could think of was
the descriptions I'd read of mass rape. People came
pounding in from all over the hospital. In one case, an
old, old lady was dying in the unit, screaming and yell-
ing. So they began to pummel and beat on her and yell
at her, and she was crying at the top of her lungs that
she just wanted to die, and they were hellbent on keeping her going a little longer. It was really terrible for me,
that assembly of people dedicated to an absolutely inhuman enterprise—all the money involved, all the talent, the machinery—to keep this poor old woman
breathing for twelve more hours, when she wanted to
die. They stole her integrity, her body dignity, all the
beauty of her life. And then she died anyway, in a terrible state, the very next day, after all that.

So I brought this up with a doctor. I said, "How do
you justify what went on here last night? When my
father was dying, at ninety-one, we had a little oxygen
for him, and he had his sons staying up night and day
with him, and he died as he had lived; he died a man.
We were holding his hand and praying with him. But
we were not going to rob him of anything in order to
keep him going. And he knew it; he knew it as acutely
as I knew what was happening to me."

So the doctor said, "You're right, it's a terrible
thing. You know, though, that there are some very tough
judgments involved."

But I said, "They're not tough judgments. You could
have gone in there with a clear conscience and turned
off all the wiring that was keeping that woman alive."
He said, "I couldn't do it." I said, "The only difficulty
would be if you had a young person in some sort of car

accident or sudden onslaught of death, and he was un-conscious—you know, *these* are hard choices. Such people live for weeks, sometimes."

Whenever an old person died, the nurses had another ritual. Everybody in the ward was awake all night, of course, listening to the screams. But ten seconds after the person died, well, they ripped the curtains shut around the other patients—because no one's supposed to see a dead body. Though in fact everyone saw everything, heard everything. While they were wheeling this poor old body out, you were not supposed to be conscious that death was going by.

It's both death-inducing and death-traumatizing. It's the fear of death and the induction of death. It's like a battlefield trying to turn into a delivery room, or some terrible thing in between—you don't know *what's* happening. You don't know what their soul is about.

This close brush with death made me think of so many things during the weeks that followed. I was thinking so much of Thomas Merton. And, of course, Bill Stringfellow—he came to see me, you know. But I was thinking especially of Merton and that electric shock that killed him. And then this absurd needle thing with me. It was strange—both of us in our fiftieth year! And both of us in exile.

LL: You certainly write about death a great deal. I'm impressed by the amount of death imagery and pre-occupation with mortality, of insistence on man's finiteness that there is in your writing. In fact, there seems to be a kind of nineteenth-century fascination with death running thematically through your books.

DB: Well, I'm very intrigued by the idea of death because I've had so much of it in my own life. Many people have died who were very close friends. Also, I've never had that kind of health, that kind of physique. And I understood those limitations in prison in a way that I never had before. The very precarious character of this whole thing. Every time I got a needle in my elbow, for example, it was very rough. I have a very low pain threshold. I don't make it too well.

LL: What's wrong with your elbow?

DB: The doctor said it's arthritis. They couldn't give me any painkillers—they just plunged that thing right in. It was murder! Right into the bone, the muscle and all.

So, there you are. I don't want to appear somber. It was just quite an ordeal. The tough thing was not going under; the tough thing was trying to screw yourself together and come back. It was very slow.

But what I'm trying to say is, I don't think I'm lacking in the energy or discipline to do what I think is right. I didn't want to start acting like a dying swan. But I really needed, from outside of prison, to be reminded of the reasons for going on. Especially at a time like that. Because things recede from you. I can't describe it, because you haven't been through it. But the reasons that would compel me to go on living weren't all that clear at that time. They came later.

I could go on once I had friends around me, especially if they were saying, "We need your help!" That's what Phil was saying. In that respect, Phil and I are so very different. He's *so-o-o* . . . very tough—

LL: So much of the living, and for the living?

DB: Yes. And also, he's so much in command of the world. You get the sense of something that has really grown out of the soil, that is really native to it. I remember that he said to me—he really has been tough on me since this happened—

LL: Tough on you? What do you mean?

DB: I mean, like laying it down. Because I have a very Zen attitude toward it all. I say, "Let it go." And he says, "No." He doesn't go for that at all. He says, "We've got to survive. There aren't that many like us around." And I say, "Well . . . I don't know." But he got me to change my job; he got me out of the dental clinic. And he made sure that I ate and exercised. He stayed on my tail. Which is good, because I wouldn't have done it otherwise.

LL: Again on the theme of death, I remember visiting you on Ash Wednesday—the beginning of Lent. In its most ancient origins, Ash Wednesday symbolized the mortality of man. At the same time, it is the beginning of the season when one meditates on the possibilities of redemption as symbolized by Christ's death and resurrection. I can well imagine that Ash Wednesday must have taken on all sorts of ironic overtones for you and your brother Philip in prison.

DB: Many parallels. It has always struck me hard that the culmination of Lent comes with a very elaborately staged kangaroo trial on early Good Friday, and then a summary execution very soon thereafter. It's really quite difficult to convey to people outside the depth of suffering that comes when, to the native helplessness of being in jail, is added this tremendous new burden—which in many ways would have been easier to bear if it had been my own. But considering all that happened in January of '71, I think we probably never experienced such a Lent as that one: the new indictments; the turndown of Phil's appeal, which meant that he must serve the full six years on his original draft files conviction; and then the turndown of our case on prisoners' First Amendment rights in Hartford.

And also the verification of my gut feeling, which has been with me for a long time, that this is not a time when you can go piecemeal after the vindication of human rights. The initiative is elsewhere; the best that thoughtful people can do is to submit before those onslaughts and make the best of it, under the supposition that either the government will go too far too fast for the public weal, or that the popular sentiment against the war will eventually turn things around against such repressive moves.

But I think that as far as we are concerned, the clue to Lent is the journey of the passion of Jesus into history, a sign that the life and death of that one man continues to signify. That is to say, it is still valid to live and die as He did. I would even go so far as to say the feeling of that Lent was that it is still valid to submit before the illegal and unhuman powers of this world, as a way of seeding something into history. And what was first true of Him can become true also for others, as long as one doesn't ask everything to be wrapped up in his own lifetime. Do you know what I mean? Any more than it was for Him. Because I think that the vindication only comes after one submits before the very real possibility of death. And there are many forms of that, one of which, I was convinced, was another trial. When I thought of going through that again, or having those I love go through that again, it was a *real* death for me. And much harder than a physical death, in many ways. Well, it was clear to me at that time that Lent in such circumstances had very tough, very deep overtones. But they were inescapably social.

And I'm not nuts about the specific reminder of man's mortality by the ashes. I think that what we need much more deeply is a reminder of our *im*mortality.

That's looking at the other end of things—that's looking at an act of God. But of course, acts of God are prepared for by men. And we have to get ready for them. I don't mean to get mystical, but I believe that those people who are worthy of immortality make themselves capable of it by their willingness to undergo death for others and to reach beyond it for others. I think that's built into living today.

At least, the invitation is there. Because the stink of death is in so many places, so many corners, so many public powers and so many methods that, even if one is almost totally unconscious, he can't get rid of that smell of death around him. The war goes on and gets expanded—right? But to be able to surmount that in a way that will be significant for others—that's the question. And I don't know, practically speaking, how one does that, except by courageously saying: "This thing may lay a claim on me, but its claim is canceled out by Christ." And I believe that. I believe that. And even though the worst happens, let me say, even though some of my friends go off to long, long periods in prison, I believe that they are accomplishing their destiny by undergoing this for the brethren. An insight that governs their own lives: weighing in one scale their own suffering and in another scale the suffering of, let's say, the Vietnamese. This puts their suffering in a better perspective and gives them a much longer view of things.

LL: How did you and Phil observe Ash Wednesday in prison?

DB: We didn't. At least not in so specific a way as by the ashes. I mean, at best the liturgy of the Church is not at pains to remind man that he is going back to dust, because that's not a reminder to man, it's a reminder to man's flesh. And ashes don't really say much about the transcendence of his spirit. That's a medieval accretion as far as I'm concerned. It was connected with a great obsession with death during the high Middle Ages. But if you go further back, to the primitive liturgy of Lent, it is a reminder that death is a stage toward immortality and that you really set your sights beyond the fate of your body if you are a *man*. So that to be reminded on Ash Wednesday that I'm bound for death doesn't say anything real to me about my human fate.

We had a second, rather more practical reason for ignoring the ashes. And that was simply that the religious scene in prison is almost entirely one of government cooptation. Invariably, the religious activity stopped dead around the altar out of cowardice and self-interest and dread of the real needs of the men. And I didn't want to identify with that kind of religion, because that's not why I was in prison. The kind of religion that impelled Phil and me to come to jail takes its start around the clues offered at the altar, but tries to end up amid the needs of real people. And those are needs that go unassuaged day after day after day by the jail priests and the ministers and the rabbis. So we had as little to do with those religious people as possible. In the name of *religion*, I might underscore, we had as little to do with them as possible. Our religious activity was our attempt to be human with the men; trying, powerless as we were, to exert some slight leverage on their behalf; so that we could say, speaking for prisoners like ourselves, "This or that situation is inhuman." And the only way we could say that was by standing there, at one with the victims.

LL: When you and Phil made a point of something like not observing Ash Wednesday, did the prisoners take notice of it?

DB: They did. The inmates were very curious about our religious lives there. For instance, we went to mass on Sunday with the men. We received Communion with them. And we did that even though we'd have liked to wear ear plugs during the sermons, and we *really* had to fight our hatred of the priests and ministers. I say *hatred* advisedly. We saw them wearing the spiritual uniform of bankrupt and corrupt power, playing that game, refusing to step aside from it even on the most atrocious occasions of human need. We'd go to one of them when a crisis occurred, and the chaplain would say, "I can't do anything. I'll have to go to the warden." And I'd say, "Does Christ go to Caesar to vindicate human need? If he does, we're in the wrong boat."

These are things that angered us very much. Why did we go to religious services at all, then? We went in order to read the gospel with the men, to receive Communion, and to be part of that humiliation.

LL: You were speaking earlier about the need for people to "smell death." Do you believe that we Americans are capable of perceiving, with that kind of acuteness, the death of those whom we are killing in Southeast Asia, either through our complicity or support? I wonder if we are even aware of our own mortality in the sense that you articulated. Isn't it possible that Americans are so locked into a materialism that invades every aspect of their lives, including their relationships with each other and their very attitudes toward human life, that they can accept the deaths of others, far away, very cheaply? I wonder if this isn't the real problem, after all, about mounting an effective peace movement based on moral issues as you are trying to do?

DB: Yes. One of the mysterious aspects of the American experience is that we're probably the first people in the history of the world who have given over our hopes of immortality to the machine. For me at least, this has atrocious implications: the idea that if your machine is powerful enough and lethal enough, it will destroy enough of the "enemies of immortality" to render you immortal. To me, this is an undercurrent of the war itself. If you can mount a death count high enough, you will have vindicated your own immortality; you will be the last man, the only one to make the future. War brings that game up-close, and technologizing the war totalizes it and makes it less and less likely that the enemy will be a survivor, or that the conflict will ever be settled outside the arena of death, settled by human compromise, by human dialogue. And so the American, quite naturally, from Kennedy through Nixon, constantly shifts the sense of human immortality from the accepted idea that all *can* survive to the idea that we alone *will* survive. Once that judgment is made, it seems to me that negotiations are knocked out in favor of the totally sensorized and computerized battlefield.

I don't want to say that this is the whole American picture, because I think that aversion to this process also runs very deep and strong. And that's part of our hope: the decency of people. On the other hand, the runaway power of this conception of the future is devastating. And Nixon is exploiting it to the hilt. You come back with a start to the idea that Chomsky speaks about so often: map out a battlefield, sensor it so that no human or bug can crawl across it, and make that your real wrestling ground for the future. You've won ahead of time because your machinery is immortal, your machinery is bigger and better than the other guys'.

But if you turn from that to the Christian symbol of Lent, you find something extraordinarily modest and powerless. In the Christian view of history, the idea that counts is that the freely offered death of one man is worth more in the long run than all of the mechanized powers of hell and earth combined. This man Jesus just can't be plowed under, can't be finished off, because He so lived and died. And that invitation is issued to those who call themselves believers: to live and die in that way. So we enter, as Pascal said, into a "wager" with God. The terms of winning are by no means clear, any more than they were in the case of Jesus. And the outcome requires an incredible intervention, because the guy loses so completely; He is literally finished off.

Of course, that's an old Jewish idea too, verified in the "anawim" of the Old Testament, who are the source of the inspiration of Jesus for one of the Beatitudes, the one about "the poor in spirit" who shall inherit the land. The root of that is very deep in the New Testament, in Luke's·Gospel especially. The poor man was the guy whose life was a kind of laboratory experiment; his business was dispensing with the impurities of power. Gandhi would probably be the best modern example I could think of from the religious point of view.

According to Jesus, the poor man is the one whose powerlessness calls upon the power of God irresistibly. God just has to move into the vacuum that this man has created around him. The vacuum being, as I would translate out of Gandhi, the laboratory, the experiment. Remember, Gandhi subtitles his autobiography "My Experiments in Truth." That is, he deliberately creates an atmosphere in which human crisis must occur, and in which, from a religious point of view, God must intervene, because the main agent is powerless. Gandhi stands in the middle of this crisis. Jesus stands in the middle of it. And jail is another way of seeing it, I think.

That is, you deliberately renounce all kinds of "cushions" between yourself and the pain of things. You could play a certain game, but you have renounced it. I sometimes think that this is one of the best clues I have about jail: that it may be a modern translation of the old Biblical idea that the very existence of the poor man calls God to his side.

I want to go easy here, because I think that a lot of the poor just suffer through and die without this realization. But I think we at least have had the opportunity of speaking with some of them and of acting as though the truth were true.

The older monastic form of this call of powerlessness to God became secularized for me in jail. When I heard my door locking at night, when I was counted like a head of cattle several times a day, when I saw that from a human point of view *they* defined my life as a stalemate and regarded me as a sprouting vegetable leaf, and when I saw myself refusing all this and yet having to undergo the conditions that actually, in many lives, made their method stick—then I saw a new form of the old thing. Biblically, it was the experience of the poor man, which in the Gandhian sense is a much more dynamic idea: that is to say, the creation of the experiment in which the truth might be vindicated and flourish. From the Catholic point of view, it is the secularization of the old monastic idea that you reach the perfection of God and mankind in isolation, in solitude, by suffering through a deliberate attempt to break you, both internally and in community. And my calm assessment, my calm reaction to the prison regime was, "I'm not going to be broken." Or, as they say in the basic thesaurus of prisoners: "Fuck them!"

But I think that it's only if a man's life has come a

certain distance that the question will make any sense. Who will say to the people in times like these, "The message of Ash Wednesday is that the ashes of children are on the air, are on the winds of the world, and we are all signed with these ashes; these ashes are on all our foreheads"? And that can be a mark of Cain or it can be a mark of Jesus, depending on what it means to us and how we turn our face to the mirror of the world. What we read there is ourselves. Who has branded us, and with what? Could those ashes be a mark of resurrection as well as of death for us? Does it mean anything to us that the innocent have died? And all the forms of death which knowledge and technology unite in creating, these are some of the real questions of Ash Wednesday. They are questions literally of life and death, questions of what is happening while we're talking. Because what is happening is the life and death of real people.

But the idea that one could enter through Ash Wednesday into some sort of personal purification without respect to the invisible writing on our foreheads—I find that a very dangerous, negative, un-Christian view not even worth talking about. What I really wanted on a day like that was to be anointed again with the blood of my brothers.

Now, maybe that's changing the figure. In prison, on Ash Wednesday, I wanted to be anointed with the ashes of the death of others, in order that I might share in their hope of immortality, and in order that I might share in it by my own choices, by my own actions, by the way *I* chose life instead of death day after day. And that meant that I was *some*where. It meant that my mental attitudes were not frozen in the events of my childhood, or of ten years ago. It meant for me, if I can put it concretely, that when I was most myself—and this only came in flashes—I said to myself at night, after a typical day in that madhouse, "How perfectly right and just it is that I am here! I see this as a reality that I agree with, that I enter into, that I touch, that I rejoice in, even."

I don't want to say that this happened very often. But at times I got an almost metaphysical joy from the rightness of what my life had come to. And I said that to Phil; I said, "There's not much juice in that idea ordinarily, because there's so much suffering around, but you do get an epiphany of it at times." And he said, "Absolutely right."

I know that Phil, under indictment on Ash Wednesday, living a much more difficult and obscure life than I, was also capable of saying that. When the indictments came down and it was clear that he was in the soup and I wasn't, at least for a time, this is the way we talked. I remember those days—I can't say I would want to go through them again—but I can remember also his saying, "This may be the time when we are being taken at our word. Maybe there is going to be no other end to this. Maybe one or both of us is going to be asked to go the whole way."

LL: What do you mean, "the whole way?"

DB: That perhaps you just never get out of a place like prison. And that they do "win," and you do indeed "lose."

These things are almost too difficult to talk about. But it's a little easier now than it was then.

5

LEE LOCKWOOD: While you were at Danbury, there was a hunger strike which resulted in your brother and several other prisoners being sent to Springfield, Missouri, for a month. How did the strike come about?

DANIEL BERRIGAN: It really goes back to June 1971 and the hearing at which Phil and I were denied parole. That's what triggered it: a feeling on the part of many prisoners that the decision was outrageous. Of course, the denial touched most intimately on the young resisters.

Then it became apparent that there was some interest outside the prison. (Nothing definite had happened inside yet.) Liz McAlister proposed, at one of the weekly defendants' meetings at the prison on the new conspiracy charges, that there be a vigil at the gate. That idea was well received by the outsiders. Then about ten of the young prisoners, most of them resisters, made up their minds that it was meaningless to hold an outside protest unless prisoners also got involved. Everything was decided in one week; everything composed and printed, et cetera; the amount of work that got done was really incredible. The most beautiful part of that early stage was the unanimity of the people who came together. Things meshed beautifully and very quickly. I take it as having been the fruit of a lot of discipline, a lot of work all year, because those who initiated the strike were mainly people involved in our classes. The authorities had made the sovereign mistake of allowing our sessions to be loaded with high-class people who were like timber waiting for a match.

We had three demands: the fulfillment of parole, a federal investigation of the whole parole system, and an official investigation and ending to the tiger cages in South Vietnam.

The first group went out about August second, a Friday. They distributed the leaflets in the yard at eight o'clock in the morning, when hundreds of people were falling out to go to work. The strikers were stationed around the yard, at points of maximum exposure, and gave out these statements and were very quickly apprehended. But there must have been two hundred leaflets given out, and I'm sure everybody read one before the day was over.

So they marched the first wave off to solitary, and of course everything was out by then—the outside publicity was already started. So things hottened up very quickly, and the difficulty of moving a second wave was somewhat greater. The authorities were expecting something to come down; luckily they didn't know what.

This was something we'd never counted on. We had counted on a certain impact, but not on other inmates standing with our people, at least not until the third or the fourth wave, if at all. But the authorities arrested Phil, and when they saw the effect of that, they panicked. The only thing that saved the place from violence at that moment was that the guards were sluggish. They are unarmed, and it took them a while to get the clubs out. And they conducted Phil to solitary without striking him. That was lucky for them.

Now there were hundreds of people standing at the entrances to their living quarters. And they wouldn't move; they wouldn't go to work, and they wouldn't go back inside. For about a half-hour, people just either sat or stood there, and a deadly silence overtook the whole yard. Then the lieutenants withdrew, and the planning sessions began. In an hour or so, they came around again, hassling the people into the houses and telling them that whoever didn't get to work would be locked in. So numbers went both ways.

Now it was about nine o'clock, and they had a couple of hundred people who wouldn't go to work locked in the houses. So they started through the houses in waves, taking names and giving people one last chance: work or solitary. At that point, it narrowed down to what in my estimation was a miraculous number: thirty-five or forty who opted for solitary. The others went back to work.

Meantime, on Sunday, they had moved the five original fasters out of the "hole" and into the prison hospital. They locked them into five rooms up there, the pretext being they they needed special medical care because they were fasting. The real reason of course was a public relations stunt. It was also somewhat of a deterrent, because those men were now under much closer scrutiny.

LL: Were they also watching you? They must have expected you to do something dramatic also.

DB: Yes. On Monday, they locked everybody up in the houses again at noon. They wanted to clear out the final untidy remnant. I had been locked in my house for about a half-hour when a lieutenant came through. And this is the way they solved *my* case: they said, "You're wanted in the hospital." They had suddenly gotten the bright idea that this was a good time to give me a physical exam, because of all the publicity about my health, et cetera. So they gave me this quick rundown—it took about half an hour—going from blood test to weight, et cetera. And by the time it was over, they had opened the houses again, so they just let me loose, left me alone and never called me out again. Phil and I were never touched, never searched, never questioned. All weekend long they were calling in elements of the whole prison community: Puerto Ricans, blacks, factory workers, outside people, all kinds; but they never came near us.

By the weekend, they had locked up the mimeograph machine and were harassing people in the education department. It was getting much more difficult to organize, but I was still able to move around and see people, and another statement was gotten ready in the Spanish language counseling nonviolence and urging a work slowdown and a food strike, also urging the three original demands. One helluva time with that statement! It was supposed to come out Wednesday night, but on Wednesday all hell broke loose and ultimately it never was issued. We would have had to hand-print the copies this time.

I saw Phil on Monday and then again on Wednesday

—imagine!—the day they shipped him out. My brother Jim had come from the Virgin Islands with his wife—we hadn't seen them in months—so Phil and I had a visit which ended at four P.M. And immediately after they got him back upstairs, they started preparations for shipping him out. I was out in some obscure corner of the yard talking to somebody, when a kid came from the hospital, one of the orderlies, and said they were locking everybody out of the hospital and the place was filthy with marshals. Something was obviously up.

By now they had locked everybody out of the hospital, and the whole area was guarded, including the inner door leading from the compound. When I came to try to find out what had happened to Phil, they just waved me away. They took all eleven fasters out about five-thirty, the usual time when they locked everybody in the houses for the count. They took them out in several cars, with shackles on, and they carried Jon Bach out on a stretcher because he wouldn't cooperate. The guards had drawn guns, all the prisoners were shackled, and there was a car filled with armed marshals between every two cars of prisoners. Ridiculous! They sped them out to the airport and flew them off, and that was it.

LL: Was the strike a success, from your point of view?

DB: In the first place, anyone who knows Danbury prison knows that the really miraculous thing was that anything happened at all. Given the short-term sentences, the high sensitivity to personal welfare, getting a "short bit" over with, as they say, and the percentage of snitches and rats who were in prison to rip off others and who keep their antennae out for anything happening —given all this I was amazed that any prisoners at all responded at that time.

LL: It's also quite unusual that in a prison, where there are, as you say, many people for whom snitching is a way of life, you were able to keep something like that quiet until it happened.

DB: The advantage was that everything, from decision to deed, took place in one week at the most. We knew that we would have to peak and finish it off quickly if it was going to happen at all, because every hour we delayed, we increased the chance of a leak. Then, of course, we all knew and had tested one another over a long period of time, in a lot of circumstances. And at the most there were only eleven people who actually fasted; for the first thrust, only five.

LL: How many inmates finally got involved in the strike?

DB: It's hard to judge, because it went in waves. But I would say that there were hundreds of men shaken by the thing personally because of their friendship or admiration for those involved. Of course there was also a certain amount of negative feeling. Some of the men thought that we were playing with them for our own well-being. At least, the accusation came forward that the Berrigans were using the parole thing and using other prisoners in order to get themselves freed.

LL: That would imply that you and Phil had some instrumentality in the strike.

DB: Phil of course took part in it. The only reason I didn't was that my friends wouldn't let me. I was all set to go. But actually, as I look back, it would have been foolish. You don't help anybody in a crisis if you get sick in the middle of it. And the authorities would have scored a big point if they could have carried me out on a stretcher to the hospital and then said, "We're giving him very good treatment—again."

I don't think I've described to you the terrific anger that I felt when they shipped Phil out that way. I was furious, but I was also trying to figure out how to make this thing useful. Finally, I decided I should write the warden a letter. I figured that he very seldom got a letter from an inmate—maybe he got anonymous letters or hate letters, I didn't know. But perhaps he never got a straight-on letter about something he had been party to. So I gave it a few days and then wrote out a rough draft and then a good one. I was struck by the fact that so much of the meanness that was visited on prisoners originated from Catholics.

LL: The administrative hierarchy of Danbury is primarily Catholic?

DB: The warden's a Catholic, the captain's a Catholic, three of the five lieutenants are Catholics, the head of parole's a Catholic, it goes on like that. Oh, yes, the whole crowd is Catholic, a cozy little counterpart to the FBI! So anyway, here is the letter:

LETTER TO THE WARDEN OF THE DANBURY PRISON

Thank you for accepting this note. I wish to review events of the last few days, and offer a few suggestions.

One grows resigned to a certain degree of cruelty in prison; still, each new instance comes with a new shock. I am told that the guards, guns, and chains used to transfer a priest and ten other nonviolent men were fit for a gang of killers.

Again, would it have seriously interfered with your "plans" if I had been allowed to say goodbye to my brother?

Mr. Norton, I have been a guest in your hostel

for just one year. A certain experience of your style entitles me perhaps to offer a suggestion to you and the other Catholics on your staff, especially to Mr. Noon and Mr. McDonald.

It is by now clear that the duplicity, cruelty, and moral inertia which are your usual methods against prisoners, must now be turned against priests as well. All to the good. I now speak to you as a priest. And I urge you—stop calling yourselves Catholics. Stop practicing religion in a way which is an abomination in the eyes of God—devotion on Sunday, breaking human lives all week. Concentrate rather on your "jobs." In such a way, you will at least be acting consistently. But do not deceive yourself any longer by thinking you can worship God and destroy men.

The work you do is simply without human meaning. It serves nothing, except your own interests. But as far as the inmates are concerned, you are only keepers of the keys in a human zoo.

How then could your religion not be in violation of the command of Jesus—"Love your enemies, love your brothers."?

But if you were to cast off this vile "religious" pretense, perhaps your children would one day thank you for refusing to live a lie. They might say of you, at least he did not mock God, worshipping Christ yet crucifying Him in his brothers.

There is no one of you who does not know I am speaking the truth. You know that you are neither rehabilitating men, nor treating them with dignity, nor helping them to change their lives. You know that you are pawns in a system that amputates men from family and community, embitters and saddens them, weakens their hope, exploits them with slave labor—and so embitters them that a majority of them return to lives of crime. In this crime, you bear large responsibility. I tell you so before God.

Of course, another alternative is open to you. You might simply quit your jobs because you wish to be men. In such a case, your religious problem would be solved.

I have a true story to close with. A friend, a distinguished rabbi, told me that in his native city in Poland, the Germans had built an extermination camp for Jews. Each Sunday the townsfolk could see the buses arriving to take the Catholic personnel to Mass. Then they would return to the camp for their week's "work." The rabbi added that it was not until he met my brother and me that he realized Catholics could be different: different, i.e., than destroyers.

You might wish to ponder this story.

In any case I am your prisoner, and proud of it. I wish you could be as proud of your lives, before God. If I were in your shoes, I would fear His wrath.

LL: Did the warden ever reply to you or say anything about it?

DB: No.

LL: I suppose it isn't the kind of letter that he could easily respond to. It reads more like an attack than a communication.

DB: Well, I thought that those big sticks would be bowled over by it because they had never heard of this type of Christianity before. I just wanted to be definite without being vindictive. I didn't want to attack them. I wanted to announce the gospel, because they had never heard it.

They knew many of the facts; but they'd never seen

them from this perspective, and they'd never had them presented by a priest. No least note of unpleasantness or uneasiness had ever entered their lives because of their religion. I think that for them it must have been like getting a note from the moon, like being reproached for not being a good moon-man. Do you know what I mean? Another planet being heard from. I had hoped that maybe they would have the courage to do a little reflecting on it. But, in fact, as far as I could see, they ignored it.

LL: During the time you and Phil were in Danbury did you have any official contacts with the Church or with your orders?

DB: We both did. Our own superiors came to see us frequently. Mine came almost every month and Phil's not quite as often. I think at the point when we went to prison, our superiors were quite anxious to keep the lines open. I think they were humanly concerned, moreover, and I suspect also that they were pressured into these visits by the younger priests and seminarians of both orders, who were always asking them questions about us. So in a remote sense the visits were satisfactory, in the way that all official contacts are; which is to say, not very.

LL: But at least these visits, however juiceless, must have been a lot more satisfying to you than your relations with the official Catholic chaplain of the prison.

DB: That's certainly true. The interlocking directorate that existed between religion and prison authority can be illustrated by the following story. An invitation arrived, I think through Bill Cunningham, to baptize in prison the newborn child of a Vietnamese couple who were friends of Eqbal Ahmad. I thought an enormously powerful moment was implied by this invitation, and I was very anxious to have part in a ceremony that would set this symbol in motion for myself and others.

In any case, the invitation shortly got lost in the bureaucratic maze at Danbury. The request got chewed up between the administration of the prison and phone calls between the prison and Washington and the religious bureaucracy—the bishop being involved and the parish downtown and the prison chaplain and so on. As was usually the case when a prisoner was involved, the only news to reach me was a negative answer; that is to say, "Forget it." No reasons, no explanations of the decision. This was par for the course.

Some months later I thought it might be good to approach the chaplain and at least find out his version of the story and his feelings about the refusal. So one morning after mass I approached him on the subject. I was met by his blank stare, a classic one, which was his typical response to all prisoners, especially when any decision was required that would demand balls on his part. He said, as I recall, that the decision had been reached "by chancery" that no baptism could occur in prison. When I inquired as to his own feelings on the decision, he suddenly, in a rare and unexpected flash, burst out in anger. It was a moment of truth, a moment of importance for both of us. First of all, it proved that he had some temper left, some reaction to me; then it showed, I think, his deep cowardice and contempt for the prisoners.

He said to me, "I concurred in this decision; I agreed with it completely." And when I inquired as to why, "Because prison is no fit place for a child's baptism." Then he yelled out again, as I recall, something like, "Baptisms belong in Church, and prisons are prisons." So I wondered mildly aloud whether or not he thought

Calvary would have been a fit place to have a mass, and then walked away. But the encounter revealed a great deal about the seven or eight years that he had spent there lazing his life away, hiding out from the pain of the prison. It had a great deal to say also about his only expectation, which was to get out of that job and into retirement unscathed, with his pension check intact. Enough said on that score.

LL: What did you think would have been the value of having the baptism occur in prison?

DB: It was related to a general feeling I've had ever since my trip to Hanoi in 1968 that the crossing of all kinds of forbidden lines into forbidden territory is a great part of the work of peacemaking. In our prison, there were inmates condemned because they had opposed the war. To bring in a child of the "enemy," in an act of reconciliation and of community, would have been to draw upon a very ancient symbol of the unity of all mankind. All the ironies of prison and free and war and peace and violence and nonviolence and poverty and affluence and waste and care of things and people, all these things would undoubtedly have been in the air, in words and gestures and actions; birth and rebirth, and death and life. All the things one has to draw upon or to dread in times of war would have been present in such a ceremony, in however hidden and anonymous a way. And I wanted very much to be a part of the exploitation of those sacred resources.

LL: Is there any restriction in canon law or in Church practice about where baptisms may be held?

DB: No, there's no official restriction either as to place or as to persons. The chaplain had made the decision and recommended it to higher authorities. So he showed his own deep contempt and dread of prison as a scene in which human life could be honored and new life welcomed. To him, quite simply, the prison was a place of desolation and death, and he came there unwillingly each day in order to punch the same clock and the same faces as the guards were occupied with, and then to flee again to safe territory. I think he felt that the same curse lay upon that place as lay upon Cain and all deviants and criminals afterward. Prison was simply not a place in which good men or women should be found after dark; and the darkness was daylong as well as nightlong.

LL: Is it possible that he also partook of the traditional attitude that one goes to jail for punitive reasons, and that the celebration of something like a baptism is the kind of privilege which criminals should be denied as part of their punishment?

DB: I think so, and of course his definition of criminal included Phil and myself. Therefore, the idea that we should be the ministers of new life, or should interpret or celebrate it, was not just bewildering to him but outrageous to his brand of Christianity. In his thinking, we were more guilty than the ordinary criminal, because we had betrayed a greater trust; we had brought down a nobler profession and cast a stain upon the Church itself—and even upon him, I suppose.

You see, under the guise of invoking the law against us, what he was really invoking was his own deep fears about changes in the Church. For him, we were a kind of noisome presence of all these changes, up close. There we were; and the fact that we were there and were surviving there and were rather constantly angry at him meant that his life was assailed at a very deep level. What he found in us was something unholy, in contrast with the rather pitiful holiness that he had always felt in himself.

On another occasion in the early winter, I think sometime in November 1971, it was announced that the bishop of the diocese was to appear on a Sunday morning to offer mass for the prisoners. The chaplain told me ahead of time that the bishop would be spending overnight in the area and that he was coming out in the morning only for mass and perhaps a short period to greet prisoners afterward. But the irony, as it developed, was that the chaplain had made it clear that the bishop was surrounded by a good deal of time before and after the mass, which time of course was not to be allocated to prisoners.

In any case he arrived the next morning: a short, cherubic, full-moon-faced man. It was my Sunday to serve at the mass, so I was the first to greet him in the sacristy behind the stage of the auditorium as he came in. And he vested, and he seemed very friendly and greeted me warmly.

LL: Were you surprised at that?

DB: No. By then we were prestige items, and he would have lost nothing by such a greeting. So we proceeded out to the mass. And he gave a sermon about a recent trip of his, which was listened to with deep respect and attention by the prisoners. He had recently returned from Rome where he had attended the ceremonies of beatification for a priest—a prisoner under the Nazis, a Franciscan named Maximilian Kolbe. Then he had gone on from these moving and momentous ceremonies into Poland to pray at the birthplace of Kolbe. So here was the bishop at Danbury to tell the prisoners about this event in his life, which had evidently touched him deeply.

There were several points of interest in the sermon that went beyond, let's say, the folkloric or the merely religious. First of all, Kolbe was a genuine hero by all accounts; his life had been subjected to minute scrutiny by the congregation in Rome before he was declared eligible for sainthood. A crisis in his career had led directly to his death. The Germans had a policy in the camp where Kolbe was incarcerated that if anyone escaped, hostages would immediately be taken and executed. On a given occasion a man did escape, and the line-up followed; every tenth prisoner was eligible for execution as the countdown was made. Kolbe was standing immediately next to a prisoner who was so chosen and pulled out of the line. And this man broke down pitifully and declared that he had a family, Why should it be he? And so on. So Kolbe immediately requested to see the commandant and offered himself as a substitute for this man. And they acceded; he was chosen for an experiment in which a number of hostages were to be simply starved to death.

So he eventually died. Of the ten who were so chosen, he lasted the longest, even though he was in very weak health at the time. So Kolbe literally died for his brother; that was the very moving lesson that the bishop brought back to us from Germany and Rome.

Well, the bishop and I repaired after mass to the sacristy and were joined by Phil, and the bishop greeted *him* warmly. Now, before the service, some of the Catholic prisoners had asked me to request of the bishop a certain time with them after mass in order to discuss some aspects of life there, especially the religious situation and the Catholic chaplain. So I made that request, and the bishop fluttered his eyelids and declared that he had no time to meet with them. This after the chaplain had unwittingly revealed that he would be spending the whole afternoon downtown in some rectory!

Then the bishop suddenly said to Phil and me, "Can you spend a little time with me?" And I said, "Like doing what?" And he said, "Well, we're going to have some coffee and meet with the officials of the prison." At this point I was angry and distressed. I said that evidently he didn't understand our position as prisoners, that we would only meet with him in the company of the other prisoners as previously requested. And, since this was not his arrangement and his wish, so long. And we left. And he went from Kolbe to breakfast with the warden and the captain and the Catholic chaplain and the other keepers.

In the days that followed, Phil and I marveled at the blindness of this man, coming from Kolbe's tomb and being unable to bear with anything except the dead; automatically aligning himself with the same powers who had produced the martyrs; coming from the honoring of a dead prisoner to the dishonoring of living prisoners.

LL: I take it that to you, the bishop represented the indifference of the Church toward such questions, in this country at least.

DB: Yes. He was an American bishop, which is to say he was a good Nazi, and he was repeating history with a blindness that we could only marvel at. I think it was a great factor in helping us understand many things—about the Church, about the state, and about that perennial agreement between the two which produces the death of good people in all sorts of arenas. And we felt a kind of desolate satisfaction at being rightfully where we were, this being correct for the times. Again, we had a new way of understanding the fact that most of the resisters wouldn't have gone in there to hear him—they didn't that morning—and that if they had, their predictions would have been verified once more. So the Church is dead—long live the Church.

LL: Why did you not stay and try to confront him with this accusation?

DB: Other prisoners were outside. If we had walked off in that little procession toward the officers' mess hall in the company of the warden and the others, it would have been kaput for anything we stood for and anybody we stood with in that prison. It was simply impossible.

LL: They would not have understood?

DB: It would have been a little like going into *Playboy* magazine to explain the exploitation of women. Such acts imply an initial corrupting decision that corrupts everything that follows. There are certain points of your life, and they're not many, in which you say "I stop here. They may go in their direction, but I'm not going with them to explain where I am, whether they understand it or not."

Even if there had been no prisoners witnessing, we could not have gone with those officials after all we had suffered at their hands and all the other prisoners had suffered. We could not have sat down at that table without destroying everything that had gone before. So our explanation to them was our refusal to go with them.

I want to relate one other anecdote about religious activities at Danbury which I think is of interest to our discussion. This took place around the time of Passover in the spring of '71. A young rabbi had been coming in throughout that year and conducting a discussion group with the Jewish prisoners on Saturday afternoons, about every third Saturday. It evolved that he was going to be in charge of the Passover Seder, and he was anxious that those of us "goys" who had become a part—or so we thought—of the Jewish community during that winter should be invited to the Seder meal and have some part in it. He wanted it to be fairly easy and informal and free-flowing and to reflect as far as possible the interests and concerns and hopes of prisoners, to be something that would arise from our own lives there.

But another current very quickly made itself felt as this traditional feast approached. It developed that, in the minds of some of the middle-aged Jewish prisoners, there was a sharp distinction between our attending a discussion group sponsored by the Jewish community and our suddenly showing up for Jewish worship. They weren't about to buy the latter and made it quite clear that they wouldn't. So a crisis arose on that night which we could help only by staying away, since we were not about to disrupt any community that had gathered on religious grounds.

LL: You had planned to take part in the Seder?

DB: Yes, to the point where I had composed a psalm, as had been suggested, and I was prepared to read it on that night, when suddenly the word came down with only hours to spare that we had been disinvited from the banquet.

This was one example of the split in religious communities that we became accustomed to. That is, there was always this old-young divergence of view about religion, about the connection between worship and life. In the Catholic community it wasn't at all as sharp, because young Catholics didn't bother going to Church at all. But among the Jews, because the Jewish rabbi pretended to a liberal, even a pacifist, background, these difficulties were rather continuous, especially in the beginning. Many of the young Jewish prisoners were anxious to connect with the religious community and would have done so if the rabbi had shown some courage. But he never had. For instance, he had allowed some of them to remain in solitary over the Jewish feast days rather than mount a protest. In this way, he had already alienated a large number of our friends months before this particular Seder.

LL: What was your reaction when you found out that you'd been disinvited?

DB: I was deeply disappointed. There was a wave of protest among the younger Jewish prisoners when they suddenly realized that Phil and I were outside, not allowed to come in. Some were for disrupting their own service, but they eventually decided not to. I was glad that it turned out the way it did. I don't think that the issue was that important; it undoubtedly would have deeply disturbed the religious feelings of some of the older people there, without any gain as far as I could judge.

A feature of that Seder that made it a particular disappointment for me was that it was the first anniversary of the freedom Seder by Arthur Waskow at Cornell in 1970, where I had made my appearance and disappearance; the drama of that night had so entered my memories and my understanding of the Testament. And it seemed to me that there was a strange new twist to the thing on this second Passover of this period of my life. That is, the Jewish community in the Seder at Cornell had been the symbolic authors of my freedom, they had helped me place the notion of going underground in the massive religious context of the Testament and the Prophets. Then, ironically, it was the second Jewish community, the community of prisoners, that refused to invite me into that same symbolism, which, I am convinced, would have been mutually liberating for both sides. But I was forced to conclude that they simply weren't ready for that kind of freedom, either for me or for themselves.

In any case, this is the psalm that I composed for that night. It's meant to be a dialogue between the congregation and the reader, and it has a refrain: "Blessed be the Lord the God of Israel."

Blessed be the Lord the God of Israel who has
   brought us to this time and place to
   remember why this night is different from
   all other nights
Blessed be the Lord the God of Israel who has
   brought us to this place, a place of enslavement and sorrow, a place of forgetfulness
   in order that we might remember.
Blessed be the Lord the God of Israel
To this place, a place of lamentation and upheaval,
   a place where families and friends are dis-
   rupted, a place of amnesia
Blessed be Thou
In order that we might remember, setting your
   gracious purpose against the purpose of man,
   against the suffering of our brothers and sisters, the enslavement of solitary confinement,
   of labor without wages, of tears and of despair.
Blessed be the Lord
That we might remember, that we might set the
   power of your mighty deeds against the pre-
   tentions of man,
That we might remember our brothers and sisters
   who languish in prison here and elsewhere;
   who, for no reason known to decent people,

suffer in kangaroo courts, in tiger cages, in
refugee camps, in torture chambers, in inter-
rogation centers

Blessed be the Lord the God of Israel

That we might remember our brothers and sisters, for the remembering of them is literally
the re-membering of ourselves; the stringing
together of our dead bones and the fibres of
our persons, the making of whole men and
women from amputees, the calling of the
breath of God to the scattered bones of the
plain; Lord, that these bones might live.

Blessed be the Lord the God of Israel

That we might remember ourselves, embracing
that larger hope, that plenary body of mankind that has lived, is living and shall live.

Blessed be He

That we might join ourselves to the heroes, martyrs, and prophets of our history who have
vindicated your word in the teeth of death,
who have defended the rights of the helpless,
sheltered the victims of war, called the mighty
to accounting, spoken the truth to power, and
died that others might live.

Blessed be the Lord

That we might join ourselves to those men and
women now living, whose lives are a long lone-
liness, who are peacemakers in time of war,
who hunger and thirst for justice, who are
meek of spirit before reprisals, who are poor
among the wasteful and slack, who are pure of
heart before the licentious, who endure per-
secution and calumny for your name's sake.

Blessed be the Lord the God of Israel

That we might join ourselves to the unborn also,
whose fate lies in our hands, whose world will
be polluted and wasted, or renewed and fruit-

ful according as we choose on their behalf, or
according as we refuse them.
Blessed be the Lord the God of Israel
That in this time and place we might join
ourselves to the unborn, who will bless or
curse us according as we choose life or death,
according as we press into their hands plough-
shares or swords, according as we draw into
unity the tribes of the earth or scatter among
them the seed of the seed of the seed of Cain,
who murdered his brother in secret.
Blessed be the Lord the God of Israel
That we might join ourselves in this time and
place to the unborn; by granting space here
and now to children, to the innocent, the victims, the outcasts, the prisoners, the exiles,
the terminal patients, the mentally ill and displaced, the old and handicapped, the helpless
and rejected, the widow and orphan—all that
vast company of the *anawim*, who are your
chosen ones, who are each and all finally ourselves; since each reveals to us the truth of our
poverty and affliction as we stand before you
Blessed be the Lord the God of Israel
Here and now, to this time and place, that we
might so live as though tomorrow were possible, as though tomorrow were probable, as
though tomorrow were actual
Blessed be He
Which is to say, as though tomorrow were neither
prison nor hospital nor charnel house nor battlefield nor pollution of air, land and sea.
Blessed be the Lord
As though tomorrow your promise were brought
nearer, because we so live that today your
promise is brought near, as near as our brothers and sisters, as near as their tears, as near

as their step—and the small reach of our love were the outstretched arm of your power, as indeed it is.

Blessed be the Lord the God of Israel

As though tomorrow were our liberation, because today we are free

As though tomorrow were the peace of mankind, because today we are peaceable

As though tomorrow had banished all pride of place, all suppression by institutions, all enslavement of poverty, racism and discord; because today we live for others, for God, for peace and decency.

Blessed be the Lord the God of Israel

Let us pray:

> Lord God of Israel, who freed our fathers from the slavery of human tyrants and called them forth from exile in the strength of your promise
>
> Free us also from sloth of spirit, forgetfulness of mind, and corrosion of will
>
> That we may gird up our lives into a single purpose and set forth in fidelity to your word
>
> One people, one heart, one purpose,
>
> Into a land which you, in good time, will show us.
>
> Amen.

LL: Amen. That's quite beautiful. I wish that the psalm could be read at every Passover Seder this year.

I think I should mention that by coincidence—or perhaps not by coincidence—today, as we are speaking, it is again the first day of Passover. That is, exactly a year has elapsed since the time you wrote that psalm. And furthermore, that we are approaching Good Friday and Easter Sunday again.

I wonder if you find it only a coincidence, or if you see any symbolism in the fact that the trial of your brother and his friends in Harrisburg is drawing to a close, a kind of passion play that may very well end on Good Friday?

DB: One of the scenes that remains in my mind from my recent visit to the Harrisburg courtroom was the judge's earnest exchange with the jury about whether or not they were to work on Good Friday. A magnificent classical irony at work here? A second meaning hidden from the main characters, revealed to those who are not blinded? Certainly, there was something very strange about a question like that: "Shall we hang these people on Good Friday, or shall we take a holiday and do it later?"

Also—speaking of passion plays—I wasn't in the court at the time, but I read an account in the paper of the first day of summation by the prosecutor, in which he confronted dramatically each of the defendants in turn, and then finally turned to Philip as the most "desplicable" among them, and made a very striking mockery of his career and life and work by deriding his status as a "peace priest." And all this in contrast to the way the court handled the prosecution witness Boyd Douglas! I think we have here the makings of a very powerful drama; it has elements of cruelty and of the absurd and of fact—of everything in modern life—played out in perhaps one half-hour of the trial. And it has for me, at least, clear resonances from the trial of Jesus, including the effort to destroy the meaning of a man's life in the minds and hearts of others, branding the innocent with the stigma of malefactor. And at the same time, the effort to reverse the roles of the antagonists so that Boyd Douglas would now appear somehow as one who had been faithful to human aspiration and to American hopes; *he* becomes the admirable person who arose from nothing to vindicate the claims of conscience and of country.

Well, I think it's remarkable that the trial first of all has come to a climax in such a week, and that our discussion about it should be the anniversary of the Cornell Seder and the prison Seder. Life and death and all the human factors in between are being aired in Harrisburg, this Passover, this Holy Week, this Good Friday.

6

LEE LOCKWOOD: How did you first hear about J. Edgar Hoover's accusation that you and Phil were the leaders of an "incipient plot" to kidnap Kissinger?

DANIEL BERRIGAN: Such news passes very quickly along the prison grapevine. Our first reaction was one of almost hilarious excitement and disbelief, a sense that this could not go much further, that it was so outrageous that there would shortly be found a way to force a retraction, and that our friends would rally round us— as indeed they did, very quickly.

LL: As I recall, Bill Kunstler went up to Danbury on your behalf and challenged the Justice Department to either issue an indictment or retract its charges.

DB: Right, and then Congressman Anderson came to

Danbury and did the same thing a few days later. So the gauntlet was laid down in a way that, at that time, we felt was beyond challenge.

LL: Obviously you didn't expect an indictment?

DB: No. I think the feeling on all sides was that Hoover had come out with these charges for superficial and very speedily concocted reasons, and that he would find a way out of them for himself and still get his money from the Congress, because he was very skilled at that; but that the charges would go no further. But I think that all of us, politicians and priests alike, badly judged the ego involvement and the fury and the sense of frustration on the part of Hoover that obviously went back to those four months when I was at large. Later on, we decided that our challenge may have forced his hand in bringing the indictment; that if we had let the storm pass, perhaps there wouldn't have been indictments; that they didn't really want them, but that they felt politically cornered by the sharp responses which issued from so many quarters.

LL: What do you think was behind Hoover's initial accusation? Do you think it was simply a case of his trying to get more funds and manpower for the FBI, or was he out to get you and Phil?

DB: I think Hoover's cupidity and egoism were part of it. But I think, more than that, he had some reason to dislike us, especially me, and he realized that in jail we were comparatively powerless. Also, I think at the back of his mind was the idea that, in long, long years of experience with American society, he had always been able to count on the Church as another ally in his search-and-destroy missions.

I can remember hearing thirty years ago that Hoover was joining in FBI spiritual retreats under the Jesuits, and that, though he was never formally a Catholic, he was very attached to the idea that religion was another branch of law-and-order. Then, in the last couple of years, that pattern of things had been shaken—mainly because of Phil and myself, I think, at least initially. And I have no doubt that that had been quite a traumatic thing for him, as it has been for many others: the realization that he might have to deal with a religious minority of resisters. You don't upset the habitual thinking of a lifetime without eliciting a great deal of anger.

LL: Were you surprised then, when an indictment was actually issued against Philip and his friends, and you were named as a co-conspirator?

DB: I can still remember the night when the indictments came down. The first indication Phil and I had was when one of the other prisoners, a dear friend, a black guy from New Orleans, came into my cell about eight-thirty in the evening and said that he had just heard over the radio that the indictment had been issued. We decided we would both go and find Phil and tell him. So we went over to the dining hall, which was open in the evening for cardplaying and rap groups, and found Phil just winding up a session with a small resisters' group. We hailed him aside and then went walking in the bitter cold of the yard and gave him the news. That night, all three of us felt as though a needle were stuck in our hearts. There was very little to be said to one another, so we circled the yard a couple of times in silence. Then Phil peeled off and went in alone and, I guess, wrestled most of that night with the burden and the future. In the morning he seemed very much as usual.

Our feeling was not so much one of surprise as of very deep shock. I was amazed at being dropped from the indictment after having been named as one of the spectacular leaders in the first announcement. And then I also had the feeling that, in a strange way, we were almost back where we began, when Phil poured the blood, and I was still not with anything that dangerous.

It struck me too that the indictment was part of a continuing effort to distract people from the main issues that are before all of us who still claim to any decency. The first issue being the war itself. It seems to me that there's a certain kind of progression here. There was, and still is, a move on to destroy what's left of the nonviolent peace movement. Some of the most viable people involved in that movement had been Catholics. They had taken the most risks; they had, I think, been the most imaginative; and they had also had the discipline that allowed them to continue their work and their communities over quite a period. So they were obviously targets for charges like these.

LL: Was there any truth to the charge about kidnapping Kissinger and blowing up tunnels in Washington?

DB: The *truth*, it seems to me, is that in times of public crisis, people discuss all sorts of things. Kennedy discussed the assassination of Castro at one point, for instance, and I'm sure all sorts of discussions go on at the Pentagon about how large the next air strike will be. One can only hope that discussions like that would end with some sort of improved sense of things.

As far as I'm concerned, such ideas may have come up in discussions and some people may have thought about them seriously, and then said "No." Certainly by August or September of 1970, people had said "No" to such tactics. Yet in some way or other these discussions became, in the hands of the government, evidence of an absolute decision. At least they wanted to present it as such. The conspiracy angle in itself is so shabby and vague that it can cover the most innocuous discussions among friends, especially at a time when peoples' nerves are rather frayed and when they have a sense of having tried everything.

LL: What about the idea of a nonviolent citizen's arrest—what do you think is the possibility of carrying off something like that?

DB: Well, as I've said often, I'm against the idea in principle because I think it's uncontrollable in a violent society, first of all; and secondly, because it moves a little bit too close to violence against the person to suit me. If I had been in on serious discussions of this kind, I certainly would have registered that opinion.

LL: You don't think it could be brought off in a non-violent way?

DB: If it's possible, I'd love to hear how.

I think another angle that must be considered is that an act like this, once it happens, gets into the society itself. And it's received in very different ways by different people, some of whom would be willing to try very violent things. That is why I would be afraid of the consequences of it in the hands of others, even though I would trust those who would so act if they were of my community.

LL: You mean that, even if it could be done non-violently, it might, because of misinterpretation, lead to acts of violence by others?

DB: It might lead to acts of the same kind by people who wouldn't have the same scruples as we would about violence to persons.

You see, I think that if we're serious, we're not talking about individual acts anyway. We're talking about actions that issue from communities that are nonviolent in principle, that are very sensitive to human rights, even in regard to people who habitually violate human rights themselves.

We're trying also to communicate with the society rather than to turn it off, a society that is riddled with wounds of violence. We're trying to say, "We have something different to offer you."

Well, as I say, these reflections are those of an individual who has not been in on serious discussions of that kind. I suppose you can get different reactions from others.

Anyhow, the reality of the indictment was a shock to us both. I think we both went through a very dark night there. It was one thing to write about prison when I was underground, and another to have it happen. Because, at the time when I came to Danbury and Phil joined me from Lewisburg, we both thought it was clear that we would get through this thing; we could see the other end of it. Then, suddenly, in January of '71, there was no other end to see. Only Phil was actually indicted, it's true, but I had to go through a certain amount too.

LL: Do you mean that you lost hope?

DB: I don't know whether it's more accurate to say I lost hope or that the bottom simply dropped out and I didn't see any meaning or direction for a while. It was something I had to work out of again. With Phil, luckily. But part of the mystery of all this is that, in the middle of it, your friends appear again. I don't want to suddenly sound as though I'm concocting something about friendship; I mean this as part of a life-and-death experience. One of the worst things that happens to you at a time when all power seems to be in the Man's hands is that a nightmare enters your soul. It says that you have no friends, or that your friends are surely going to give up on you now, that they really cannot bear the weight. I can remember going through sleepless nights thinking, "We've lost everything, we've lost our friends." It's a matter of broken confidence; it's a matter of not being able to believe that they can still believe in you. The way I feel now, that doesn't seem very logical; I'm just trying to say how I felt then.

When the indictment strikes, you're so unprepared, you know so little about what's coming. And then slowly, or maybe not so slowly, your friends reassemble —within twenty-four hours it happened! And you suddenly see that a nightmare that claimed to be life itself was nothing *but* a nightmare. It has dissolved. Yet, for a while, it's just like Demosthenes' cloud—no bigger than a man's hand, but it covers the sun.

LL: Of course, if you had been outside those walls when the indictment came, perhaps you wouldn't have been as much a prey to that kind of depression. There in prison you were partaking of a community of despair—

DB: All the time, all the time! And you see, it's not only that we were in such a community; it's also that our whole life there was dedicated to being a counterforce to despair. We were bearing the burdens of despairing people around us while trying to keep a certain overflow of cheerfulness and hope ourselves.

LL: How did Phil take it?

DB: I would put it this way: He never went as deep into depression as I did, and he came out beautifully. He took the whole prospect with great equanimity.

Part of the astonishing character of that man, from the point of view of the other prisoners, is that everybody expected the two of us (I say the two of us, but I mean it mostly of him) to function skillfully and normally under every circumstance. If one of us had suddenly struck somebody, or done something demeaning in public, or shown bad spirit, they simply wouldn't have believed it. And part of the reason is that they could not conceive of what we were going through. They just said, "Well, these guys, I don't know how they do it, but they do it." They really expected that a guy like Phil would always be at his best. And he invariably was. But they had no insight into what he really went through. While they themselves felt free to indulge in almost every vagary and despair and change of temperament, free also to come and dump everything on us, *we* were not supposed to dump on anybody. That's where we had to take care of one another.

LL: Was it your hope, at the beginning, that the Harrisburg trial could be conducted on a high political level, in the manner of your trial at Catonsville?

DB: Let me speak about some things that were on my mind at that time. This has to do with the ticklish and difficult question of the role of the defendants themselves at the trial vis-à-vis that of the lawyers. My thought then was that the trial ought to be as freshly thought out as though there had never been such a trial before. Every trial has to be new; and to the extent that you don't think it through again, you risk turning it into a stereotype, turning the clock backward.

One of the most exciting developments I know of is a combination of legal defense by lawyers and self-defense on the part of the people indicted. This happened both at Milwaukee and Rochester and again in the Camden trial—people decided to dispense with all legal nonsense: the liturgy, the automatic assumption of robes and roles, the implication that lawyers are automatically mediators between the defendants and the jury. My strong feeling was that things had to be thought through from the ground up again. And that lawyers in such cases as ours should never be allowed to presume that they are the chief actors or the chief interpreters of politics or the chief voice of social passion on behalf of the defendants.

Ideally, that thinking ought to descend into every practical detail, from strategy and tactics and choice of the jury, through the opening speeches, to the examination and cross-examination—right through the trial. What part do they have and what part do we have? The lawyers should retain a role which is only relatively important, a role of advocacy and advice rather than one of mediation and interpretation.

LL: Do you mean that you'd also like the lawyers to give first priority to the political questions and make the juridical questions secondary—the questions of guilt or innocence according to the law, of discrediting of the prosecution's evidence, and so on?

DB: I can't adequately deal with that. First of all, I was not a defendant, and it's pretty hard to put myself in their shoes on that question.

LL: It can't be all that hard. After all, you were in jail almost two years.

DB: This was a much tougher thing coming down on these people. There was a possible life sentence involved, according to the first indictment.

In any case, I don't see how the two questions can be separated. It's a question of skillfully and mutually penetrating those questions, the political aspects of defense and the defensive aspects of politics. One doesn't want the kind of politics that sacrifices human beings. Nor does one want the kind of self-defense that sacrifices political idealism.

LL: Suppose you found yourself in the position of having to make a choice between the two?

DB: It can't be a choice, or else the trial loses all its meaning. Practically speaking, either alternative is unthinkable without the other, unless one is willing to sacrifice the defendants or abandon the politics that brought one to trial in the first place.

The fact is that, regardless of how much experience he may have gained in the courtroom, no lawyer is charged with *these* crimes, no lawyer is in the dock. To me that's the essential difference; it's as simple as that. How do we tell about our lives, about where we are? No lawyer is where we are.

This goes beyond anything abstract. As I saw in the "Flower City" trial in Rochester, the effort to get directly to the people, whether they're jurors or audience or judge, can be a very enriching thing on all sides. It shatters the old forms. In Rochester, the judge himself was pushed into a new role. As he said himself: "Just because these people are so young and so inexperienced and yet have availed themselves of the privilege of defending themselves, I have to treat them very differently." He said that publicly. And he also said: "I have to allow much more leniency in cross-examination, in their whole style"—which he did.

LL: But what happens when you have a judge like Julius Hoffman, who responded in completely the opposite way at the Chicago trial?

DB: Well, when that comes up, that has to count too. The courts have to deal with that.

But what I think is worth working toward are these new relationships. As I could see at the Rochester trial, the jury was shaken, was turned sympathetically in a new direction by those young people, in spite of being almost hopelessly middle-American. The jurors were deeply touched by those defendants; obviously their verdict reflected that. All the legal acumen in the world remains just that in the minds of jurors—legal acumen. And the more skillful it is, in a sense, the more dangerous it is, because people begin to ask, "Is this a show, or is something sincere coming through?" But if you're confronted with the defendants themselves, no such questions arise. In a much harder, up-close way jurors have to decide whether or not these people are genuinely saying something about the future of their country.

LL: I suppose that a trial, like a liturgy and like many of the hardened forms that we have in our culture, is in the final analysis a way of avoiding ideas and feelings rather than of transmitting them. And perhaps breaking those forms down is the only way to refresh their sources and bring them back to what they were meant to be in the first place.

DB: Yes, and of course there are all sorts of ways of doing that. Some of them absurd, and some creative.

LL: Do you think the defense tactics at the Chicago trial were absurd?

DB: I think the problem existed at the other end— that they were *received* as absurd.

LL: It was a matter of bad public relations?

DB: It was a matter of the anxiety of the court and of the media to make headlines, to make them daily. Actually, the instances of courtroom disruption in Chicago, as I understand it, were minimal.

But even if, among the Harrisburg defendants, there had been any inclination to be disruptive, it would have been absurd and counterproductive from the beginning because of the wave of sympathy that had gathered around us. My hope was that people would be able to distinguish between a trial which is a stereotype and a deadly bore on the one hand, and on the other a trial that would convey a certain style and would break through the sacred and acceptable mold of the old liturgy. Somewhere in between there's room to move; to struggle toward new relationships, new ways of communicating—I think it can be done.

LL: Did you have any concrete ideas about how it could be done? You're talking in very general terms.

DB: Well, each one of those six people had had years of the most varied types of experience—in pulpits, in classrooms, on platforms, on radio and TV, in personal counseling—the variety is endless. And several of them, at least, had had courtroom experience, either as defendants or as advocates for the defense. Out of all this, it seems to me we would have been fools if we hadn't urged upon them new ways of communicating in that trial.

I can speak concretely of Phil. I have never heard any public utterance of his that didn't win a hearing, either because good will was there initially or because he created it by his manner, by his knowledgability, by his compassion. And yet, as I look back on the four trials he's been through, he's had very little opportunity to show his greatness in the courtroom. At Catonsville, he had been locked up for quite a while—I mean under real lockup, not in a place like Danbury. He came to the trial so exhausted and befogged that it was very difficult for him, even in the cross-examination, to put his story together.

But even then, there was a great difference between his ability to cope during the trial and during the sentencing. On that morning, his statement was carefully and beautifully prepared. It was so beautiful that in the Catonsville play I incorporated it into the trial account. I think it's one of the most powerful things in the play.

Remember when he calls upon judges and clergy to stand where we did? It's a splendid passage. It showed what he could do under adverse circumstances.

LL: A number of times I have heard you voice the thought that the indictments against the Harrisburg people constituted a new situation, because the "ante" was so much higher than it had been in other trials in the past. Yet it seems to me, if I have understood you correctly, that in a very important sense you *want* the ante to be as high as it possibly can be. Isn't that so? Don't you feel a certain inconsistency between what you've said before and your attitude toward Harrisburg? Of course, in a pragmatic, human sense nobody wants to go to jail for the rest of his life. But isn't it true that everything that you and Phil and the others have been doing is directed toward raising the ante of resistance as high as it possibly can go?

DB: You see, again I'm being caught here, because the ante was not being raised on *me*.

LL: It could be, at any time.

DB: The day it is, we can take up this question again.

LL: I see. In other words, you were simply speaking out of concern for your brother and your friends, and not for yourself?

DB: Exactly. I had no right to get noble and deep-breathing about them when I wasn't standing in the dock. I was acting in a certain advisory capacity with them, but my skin wasn't up for sale, and theirs was. And that's a hell of an ante. To raise the risks of Catonsville, where the ultimate jeopardy would have been five, possibly ten years, was one thing. But here, the indictments carried penalties of up to life—that's pretty heavy stuff; it couldn't get much worse.

LL: I don't mean to harp too heavily on this theme.

But it seems to me that all during the time you were underground, you were urging middle-class professional people—people not unlike those who stood trial at Harrisburg—to perform illegal acts of resistance that could involve high levels of jeopardy. In effect, you were saying to people: cross the line; break the law; raise your own ante to the point where it begins to equal the loss and suffering that is being exacted by the war itself.

This was strong language; but I never felt that you meant it merely metaphorically. Yet, isn't this exactly what the Harrisburg defendants had done, regardless of how muddily the government's charges against them were framed? Isn't that precisely why they were on trial in the first place? And if those defendants had been able to throw that kind of light on themselves—I am excepting Philip and Eqbal Ahmad from this, because I think they did see themselves that way but were overruled by the majority—mightn't they have been more willing and able to speak directly to the issues?

DB: I see certain stages in the lives of the defendants prior to the trial. During those months after the indictments came down you could have put a microscope on each of them and gotten a pretty good anatomy of the development of the human spirit under fire. Every element of growth, fear, dread and despair would stand out, and also the illness of spirit that in my experience often precedes a new leap of being.

Then there comes a period of recovery when friends can gather again and see their lives across a larger perspective. But there's still intense understanding of the threat overhead; everything that you were deeply convinced of in principle is now going to be demanded of you in fact. You've been shunted onto front stage, you're standing there under the lights speaking to a live audience. You no longer have an esthetic distance between, let's say, where your life was and where your words were.

It seems to me true even in the case of Jesus. He spoke of the necessity of taking up the Cross and following Him, of living the life of faith, all of that. And yet, at the time of His own trial, and even before, His heart really failed within Him. I suspect He also said to Himself, "Now all those words about life and death are coming true." And He was still young. And the ante had been raised to the point where everything that He had said before had to be verified in His own flesh.

That's very rough stuff, and I think it's a mercy of God that we do have the Gethsemene scene, where He's really beaten flat and bleeds at the prospect of what lies ahead.

LL: Although most of the defendants knew one another to varying degrees before the indictment, they obviously were not a unified group of people who had worked closely together and knew one another intimately. It must have been an interesting and difficult process for all of you to get together and begin to formulate a defense, especially in view of the fact that the meetings had to take place in prison because Philip was in jail.

DB: Right. And that was the task that began immediately after the indictment came down: how to make this long preparation fruitful in a human and legal and political sense, and how to arrange our thinking and our lives so that we could begin to endure the discipline of this long, long time together.

In the beginning, we decided that, once a week for about three hours, all the defendants would gather at Danbury in a room that they would set aside for us. And so we began to get acquainted again, slowly to reach out toward one another and draw a little bit closer under the common jeopardy. Of course we never knew whether or not that room at Danbury was bugged. And I think that uncertainty *also* bugged us, especially in the beginning. We knew that we had to be quite candid with one another if we were going to get anywhere; yet being in prison was such a psychological and spiritual handicap to that growth. We were always searched when others left, and on several occasions a functionary searched through everybody's belongings. I remember that on one occasion he stole a piece of bread that Liz had in her handbag for the Eucharist.

LL: Because it was "contraband"?

DB: Right. "Nothing is allowed," he said with his straight, dimwit face, "except what was bought out of the machines on the premises." So he took that good piece of bread, and I hope it turned into a stone in his pocket.

Anyway, for Phil and me those meetings were a special way of doing time. We were marking time not in the ordinary, depressed state of prisoners who were chained to a wheel in Hell. We were marking time by the faces of our friends week after week, and by the rhythms and expectations and low points that were reached at these meetings, painful and tragic and difficult and very joyous. And then having a Eucharist in a room where it was forbidden, where the wine was in a tin can and the bread had to be concealed. We even had to read the Scripture covertly.

LL: Why covertly?

DB: Because any Catholic guard would be able to put the thing together: they're reading Scripture and passing bread and wine. There was that sense of danger overshadowing the thing, from beginning to end. But again there was always the sense of the essential rightness of what we were doing, the sense that those were the best and the most authentic of the liturgies we had ever had together.

So in an atmosphere that was possibly bugged, and where there were always guards outside the room and sometimes in the room, with all these pressures, we began our work. And I would say that it went well, given everything, and that people did grow in their sense of one another. For, though we felt galled and even gagged by having to prepare in jail, still I think it had its advantages too, especially from the spiritual point of view. The defendants were always conscious of the lives Phil and I were being forced to lead there. They could sense that their fate had already begun in us, was already under way.

I think it was a sober discipline for them to return to this setting every week where the mills of the gods had already begun to grind. Even the long, long discussions that got nowhere, either because the plans were discarded then or were later shown to be unworkable, all these things were part of something greater: the effort to hold together seven or eight very diverse people. We were trying to include very different views of life and of trials and of politics and of religion, to keep afloat in circumstances that were sometimes comic and sometimes tragic, as in the sudden death of Eqbal's brother and the death of Neil's father. I think it's almost miraculous that the defendants didn't end up with separate trials or separate lawyers, or at least with a very active friction operating among themselves.

I think it should also be said in all candor that the greatest single potential factor for disruption was always Philip, and the greatest single factor for unity was also Philip. That was true for many reasons: background and character and politics and being in jail. He was also, I think, the most positive and articulate of the members, the one most closely connected to the other defendants. But he decided, very early in this whole process, that practically everything else had to be subjected to one non-negotiable project: that we work together and go into the trial together and come out together—one moral voice, one political voice, one defense. And that, as events turned out, represented great sacrifice, the greatest of all on his part. But it happened. And when I read in accounts of the Chicago trial of the hatred and friction that arose among the defendants, of the lamentable divisions in the Spock trial, I see that this was no small achievement. .

Maybe it could be argued that this dampened the kind of trial that Phil could have prepared by himself or with one or another of the lawyers. I think that this is always arguable; if some values were gained, others were undoubtedly lost. One of the deep disappointments almost from the beginning was our different views of Kunstler's role. It was extremely painful for Phil and myself that the others simply did not want him in the trial in any visible sense. And we did, we deeply did. He was visiting us all the while; he was very close to us the whole time that I was in jail. And we never diminished in our sense of Kunstler as friend and advocate, of the great loss to the trial and to our lives because he was not as deeply involved as Leonard Boudin or Ramsey Clark.

LL: What was the division on the issue of Bill Kunstler? Why did the majority not want to have him on the legal team?

DB: I think it followed from several factors. There was an element of caution among the defendants as they approached the trial, stemming from the fact that no one of them except Phil had ever been on trial before. Secondly, no one of them except Phil knew Kunstler in a personal way. Then I would say they had been more or less victimized by the events of Chicago, and the feeling that he was a spectacular egoist, that he was unreliable, that he was too far out. Their judgment upon his conduct and politics was, we felt, extremely unfair and inaccurate.

LL: Do you think that Kunstler's politics were too radical for this group, or was it more a question of their putting a priority on a legal defense ahead of political defense, of their wanting to be sure that they got the best possible legal defense regardless of politics?

DB: Well, that sort of thing may have been operating in the background, in all candor. Several of the defendants never wanted a real political priority in the trial. But I have to separate *my* sense of them from their sense of themselves, and I find that difficult, especially as their friend. I think that from the beginning they were traumatized by the indictment. It was difficult for them to face the possibility of a political trial that would put personal jeopardy up front. And this was all part of their thinking about Kunstler and about what he might do, based upon what they had heard he once did. Rumors about rumors.

LL: This seems a bit strange in the light of the fact that several of the defendants had earlier engaged in draft board actions and had announced their responsibility publicly afterward. As I remember it, they had gone into those actions with the idea and purpose that they would be arrested, indicted, and then hold a political trial à la Catonsville.

DB: What I think has to be taken into account here, from my own experience, is that rational judgments, even on the part of people involved in political jeopardy, simply don't come easily when indictments come down. One's conduct after an indictment very often follows upon a huge release of irrational or a-rational factors that one simply had not been aware of before. There is an overwhelming realization that suddenly one's life and future are up for grabs, one is no longer master of the choices that he thought really determined his life. All this suddenly has to be taken into account, and it can only be taken into account by friends who will be able to bear with the new person who emerges out of a new crisis, whose attitudes are now so different that they couldn't have been predicted.

LL: You mean, when confronted with the reality of the power of the government?

DB: Right. And the fact of jail, no longer as a remote possibility but as something that is nearing day by day. It puts one's life into a nightmarish new perspective, not only for the person involved but also for his friends. Suddenly, politics become subject to the reign of the absurd. And maybe that's the moment at which one becomes a person for the first time. Suddenly, the unconscious and subconscious in one's soul must be confronted close up. And out of that comes, it seems to me, a deeper and better mix, a person whose soul has been remade. That's the only way I can speak of these people. Especially in the light of the fact that, from the moment of the first indictment in January of '71 right up to the end of the trial, their sense of themselves has not changed much. Though I think that it had changed rather radically in the time before, between the draft board actions and the Harrisburg indictment.

LL: You don't think it was also a question of being confronted by their own naked fear at the moment when the full power of the government was suddenly revealed to them?

DB: I think it's more complex than that. No one operates independent of the events swirling around him. The progress of the war and the temporary victory of Nixonian politics and the copout of the movement from the realities that the Catholic Left was facing—all these factors created a kind of vacuum around people. They had to decide, especially in the case of the Scoblicks and of Neil McLaughlin, whether or not the courtroom could be an apt place in which to expose their lives and try to expand political understanding.

Do you see what I mean? It's not a simple matter of saying: They changed because suddenly they became fearful people. They changed certainly because personal fear had to be faced. But they also changed because they were trying to understand whether or not it was worthwhile to go forward in the way they had been summoned. They knew a noose was tightening, drawing them into court and jail. And there are various ways of dealing with that. One of them is simply to dig in your heels and say: I'm going in there unwillingly; I'm going to say as little as possible; I'm going to show my contempt by my silence. And that was the decision of some of them. So it would be unjust to reduce their politics to fear before the fact of imminent danger.

But at the same time, I have a feeling that William

Kunstler would have been a better public interpreter of their view of the law and of their lives than the lawyers chosen. But that's a personal opinion.

LL: I think it's important to draw upon the historical context that was operative in terms of where the peace movement stood at the moment that the indictments came down, and even later, when the trial took place. The time when these people were engaging actively in resistance, in draft board actions, coincided with the high point of the movement itself. That is, there was a lot going on, all kinds of resistance and protest, and there was a sense of a large, nationwide mass of people who were actively engaged in resisting the war—a real *movement*, of which they were a part. But by the time the indictment was issued, a year later, the movement had collapsed, and they felt isolated and disillusioned.

DB: Yes, and I think that was part of the terrible feeling about our lives which all of us had to deal with at the time. A sense that we had been betrayed, not so much by Boyd Douglas or the Justice Department or Hoover—after all, these betrayals were understandable—but by the movement. Neither Philip nor I would hesitate to say that, if the movement had been *moving*, the indictments would never have come down. That is, if there had been enough counterpressures of conscience and assaults upon law and property around the nation, these hundreds of idle agents and idle government lawyers would have been too busy to move in on us. Public opinion would have been at a very different point. If only we could have pushed back the atmosphere to the fever of around June 1970, that period when the whole country was aflame because of Cambodia and Kent State and Jackson State! But the fever was followed by chills, and it was in that period of chills that we ourselves almost perished.

LL: Earlier, you said that during both the Chicago and the Spock trials there developed considerable acrimony among the defendants because of the diversity of their backgrounds and personalities. I think that's true; especially in the Chicago trial there was an almost complete spectrum of personalities, political orientations and life-styles. But in contrast, the Harrisburg defendants, and I would even include Eqbal Ahmad, though he doesn't have the same Catholic resistance background, seemed a rather homogeneous group, politically anyway. So it seems surprising to hear that there was as much diversity of viewpoint among them as you suggested.

DB: I guess your question arises out of a public stereotype; you know, that all Catholics turn their noses in the same direction and follow the same whistle or buzzer or lock step or summons of conscience. I could point to the split vote that came near the end of the trial on whether or not to offer a defense as the last and latest evidence that these are very diverse people.

Actually, the struggle to retain any unity worth speaking of was a very deep one. Those people had entered into illegal actions for reasons that arose from very different backgrounds and experiences. Catholics, yes; carbon copies, no. Seeing themselves in that way, they came up toward the trial with all their individuality, wanting it respected and retained, wanting to be known not as disciples or followers of anybody, but as themselves. This was true of even the quietest and the least articulate among them. And everyone, come what may, was determined to respect that individuality.

And hard as the various tugs and pulls were, we could sit down and be silent together and read Scripture and ponder it and at least keep coming back to some sense of what lay beyond the present travail. We kept reminding ourselves that a sense of one another was all that we had been about before there were any indictments, all that we had to offer other people. And that if that sense were broken, then we had really spilled the milk, and we would have very little to offer others. I think by and large that sense of things was correct, and when the pieces have been picked up it will be seen that this was probably the best thing to come out of the trial. That people were simply not torn apart by the indictment; that the defendants could go out after the trial and take up their public lives with no great discontinuity, even though they'd been through a vicious ordeal. I wonder whether or not that could be said about other trials and other defendants? I don't know.

LL: I think that the history of these great political conspiracy trials that have occurred in recent years shows that most of the defendants were traumatized by the experience of the trial itself. But would you be more specific about what it was that Philip sacrificed, in order to help preserve the community?

DB: From the beginning, he saw the trial as a contest in which a reversal of roles must occur. That, of course, was a noble principle; and we all tried to break it down, deal with it, look at the components and put it together again over all those months. By and large, I think his view of things was shared by the others in principle. That is to say, no one felt criminal as a consequence of the charges, and all of us felt our government was criminal. But how to make that apparent during the trial became a matter of very great differences among the defendants. Philip and I felt, Eqbal and Liz in measure also, that this principle, if it was to be taken seriously, meant that the trial first of all should be a political event. That the question of jeopardy, while very real, was subject to the truth of the trial, which truth could only be released and communicated by the political sense of the defendants.

Well, that order of things was hotly debated from the early preparations right up to the end of the trial. But it became apparent, in the course of our preparations, that while the principle was shared by all, the conclusions leading from it were not by any means held in common. And that putting the principle into practice in the trial and going in there with priorities clear was bound to be a struggle. The struggle was intensified once the prestigious lawyers entered the scene and began to declare their sense of the trial, which was much more closely aligned to that of the more moderate of the defendants.

LL: You mean, more law-oriented?

DB: Yes. So all through those months, it became painfully clear that Philip's view of things was not going to prevail. That his hopes for a creative or experimental or probing trial that would proceed from day to day and take its tactics from the events of each day, all of this was receding in favor of a rather staid and traditional trial.

7

DANIEL BERRIGAN: Finally, after several delays, the definitive date of the trial was announced, and right around the New Year it became clear to Phil and myself that the day of our separation was near. As it happened, we had arranged for a final meeting of defendants on the very day they decided Phil should be hauled off to Harrisburg; we were only notified of this decision the night before. But the meeting we had scheduled had great importance for us; it was to be a climactic meeting on some issue that had come up. So the night before, after many spasms and trials and errors, Phil got a phone call out to New York, notifying the defendants that he was to be hauled off in the morning in manacles, and would they please do something about it.

Well, the morning arrived with no relief in sight, and Philip received notice to appear in front of the yard where the marshals had come in. So we went out there together, and he, still storming, announces to the associate warden that he's not leaving until the question of the visitors is settled. Finally, he is allowed to go in and sit down with the marshals while I wait and explain the reasons for his resistance to this sudden departure. And the marshals inform him that, like it or not, he's going off with them.

By this time, the scene is very hot and difficult for all of us, because the marshals always set their jaws when they believe a prisoner's going to resist them. It makes no difference who the prisoner is. Suddenly, however, the other defendants appear at the front gate. This introduces a complexity: should they haul Phil off in the sight of his friends? The scene is pure Mack Sennett; I'm trying to tell Phil what has happened, and he's trying to shout to me across all these functionaries and apes. One of them is trying to nudge me away with his broad-assed hip. Then this little conversation ensues. Ape says, "Keep your distance, prisoner!" I say, "Why can't you act like a human being? He's my brother, you know." Giving me the hip: "You seem to forget that you're a prisoner." Nothing daunted, I retort: "You forgot years ago that you were a man."

Now get this. They separate us off. Philip goes out the front door, resigned to the fact that he is to be shipped off, and I go up to my job in the library.

Some of the young resisters have snuck off their jobs in order to be with me in the library for a half-hour or so, to share the fact that Phil has gone, and gone for good. And suddenly, in the midst of our mourning, here's big Philip in the doorway, grinning like risen Jesus and saying, "Anybody got a cup of coffee here?" And we wheel around, looking for all the world like guys who'd been keeping the tomb all week. Here he is again! And we quickly drag him over—embraces, great laughter and all that. They had changed their purported minds, and we had eight hours of grace.

LEE LOCKWOOD: It must have been lonely for you after he was gone.

DB: It was bad for a day or so. My strongest gratitude was for the year we had had together, the fact that neither of us had ever dared hope we would be together in prison. It was the longest period we had been together since boyhood, some thirty years before. In all our adult lives, we had had only very intermittent meetings, the longest being a couple of weeks together on summer vacation; but never just the two of us, always with family or in a crowd.

Then, suddenly, we found ourselves together for almost eighteen months. And that was just, well, a gift of the federal government, a gift beyond belief to both of us. For the first time in our lives we were able to do some really deep thinking about the past and the way our lives would be going. Then we shared the anguish of the indictments, the preparation for the trial, all sorts of family meetings, the educational experiment, the exploring of relationships with resisters and other prisoners. In fact, the substance of our lives together multiplied beyond measure the experience that would have occurred to either of us, had we been separated in prison.

So I tried to keep in perspective the separation which we both expected to be a very long one. At that time, I still had no inkling that I would be paroled, and of course Phil was looking forward to at least the completion of his current sentence. But I was able to heal up very quickly any sense of being wounded by his departure. I felt simply that another phase was finished, for which we were grateful, and let's get on with what was to come.

LL: Because you and Philip are so closely associated in the public eye, I think it's not generally known that your careers in resistance developed quite separately, and that you weren't always working together as a team. Did you find, over the long period of time that you were together in prison, that you had different ideas about politics or resistance tactics or about other aspects of your lives?

DB: I suppose the impression could arise that we were yoked to the same chariot and moving together in the same direction. Of course that was never true at all, even geographically, though I think in other ways, especially spiritually, it was always true. I was only with Phil in times of vacation, as I said, or moments of crisis; and the rest of our communality was done by phone and letter and resonance, I guess. In our life in the priesthood, we were never even in the same city for any length of time. Even when we were both living in New York City for a year or so in the sixties, we were not on assignment together. We always had separate jobs, so that we were always meeting across diversities, which never were differences in any real sense. And I think that all this was very good—we never became shadows of one another. We were never in a disciple or follower relationship. It was always consciously mutual and complementary.

LL: Do you have a sense of being a team?

DB: I think that is one very good way of putting it. Our lives are parallel, converging, as we hope, on the real world and the real Church and real people. So our different fields of work have been very enriching for both of us. But when we came to prison, we needed time to share our very different experiences, especially after so many years. Weirdly enough, it was in prison that we caught up on the past and made it part of our future together.

And now we are separated again. There's a sense of déjà vu in the fact that I'm visiting him again in jail and in the courtroom, that I'm out again and he's not. It's new, and painful in its newness, because it's obviously not a mere repetition of the past. We're now in the air war, in the seventies and in Nixon, and I'm picking up life in a way that is very new to me, while Phil is involved in a trial that is obviously a new assault upon his life and the lives of his friends. So it's only superficially that anything could be called repetitive about this phase of our lives. And the same question recurs, the same and yet never the same: Where do we go from here? How can we give a little space to the next generation, and even to this one?

LL: You were never a defendant in either of the indictments, and you were dropped as a co-conspirator, yet you took part in all the strategy meetings and preparations. Did you feel any ambivalence with regard to how far you could participate? I'm curious to know what role you played in all of these discussions.

DB: It was certainly a complex one. But I think in practice it became very simple. What does John the Baptist say about himself in the gospel? Something about being the friend of the bridegroom; I was the friend rather than the protagonist. And that was an easy and natural role for me. It dictated that I would not initiate strategy except in a very suggestive way, and that I would not insist upon roles or tactics or anything practical except what came out of prior discussions between Phil and myself. I always wanted my voice to be one of friendship and experience and to issue also from the particular situation of jail, so that I would not be an added source of conflict, or—God help us—as they say in engineering, a "resource person." I would just hang around to listen and to suggest; and, especially in certain circumstances, I was always conscious of the weakest member or the one I felt was not being heard from, and I would try to reinforce him.

LL: Were you also a mediator?

DB: I think so, on many occasions. And, of course, I was always conscious of Phil's exposed position as the one they were really whetting their knives for, the one the government wanted with the fiercest appetite. So my being with Phil continually made it a little easier for him, I think, to sit down with the other defendants in a way that was a little more patient, because he had thrashed things out with me during the week.

LL: Why did you not want to participate more actively in planning strategy?

DB: Well, I don't think I'm particularly good at that, first of all. I think also that anything that I have to offer a scene comes out of a vivid sense of my place in it. I'm sure that if I had been a defendant, other energies would have been awakened. But in this circumstance, it was clear to me that my role was one of reinforcing or advocating, helping build people's confidence and trust in one another.

So it seemed entirely natural when I was in Harrisburg during the closing week of the prosecution in late

March that I was invited to that final conclave on the question of going ahead with a defense.*

LL: Do you want to discuss that decision?

DB: Maybe I could speak of some things that were in the air that night. First of all, Philip was not at all anxious that he win out, any more than he ever had been. He was anxious only to be heard. I sensed in him an urgency I had known as a prisoner too: people around you are mobile and available to one another, and there you sit in the middle of it all. You can get very angry, having something to offer and not being heard from. I got a little sense of that that night. And Philip made a clear distinction between the fact that he had an opinion and the fact that it was *only* an opinion. On the first score, his dignity and sense of himself was involved; and on the second score, his sense of them. So he was going to be heard from, yet he was not going to throw his weight around.

He made the point that night that the political heart of the trial had not yet been exposed; indeed the reasons that had brought the defendants to the courtroom had not yet been aired, either in the world at large or before the jury. It had been a traditional lawyers' trial, and in that sense, it had had very little meaning for him. He was quite willing to undertake all the risks that involved his own person, his future, the extension of his jail sentence by another conviction. He felt confident that the defendants could improvise a way of getting heard in the course of the defense. He wanted these facts known.

* The most dramatic moment of the trial was in some respects an anticlimax. It occurred at the conclusion of the prosecution's case when former U.S. Attorney General Ramsey Clark, a chief defense lawyer, rose and stated simply: "These defendants will always seek peace. The defense rests."

Then he wanted to be silent and hear from the others.

The opinions of the others covered a wide spectrum. There was a kind of long-term contempt for the legal scene on the part of Joe Wenderoth and the Scoblicks and Neil McLaughlin. Their attitude had been quite consistent for a year and a half. They felt that they had simply been forced into the assumption of guilt, into the courtroom and its absurd rules and regulations, into the presumption that their lives were under scrutiny by questionable powers. And they were saying "No"; they were saying "No" all along, for a year before the trial. And, while they were open to the others, it was quite clear that very little was going to be heard from them during the trial. As far as they were concerned, this was not their scene.

Eqbal's opinion stemmed from a carefully prepared paper, in the Eqbalian sense, outlining "four main points" as to where he stood. He went through them in great detail that night: the idea that there should be a defense, but a very limited defense. There should be a defense because this was the only way to speak of the life and death of the innocent, of Nixon, of the complex of violence that had hauled people into this courtroom. On the other hand, he felt that only Liz should go on the stand, because she could articulate the position of the defendants well and yet was the least vulnerable to cross-examination along the sensitive lines of draft board involvements and the specific charges about the tunnels and kidnapping. Moreover, she could speak for their position with a style that would be gentle and feminine, yet clear and strong. She would have particular appeal to the jury with minimum risk for the defendants, especially for Joe and Philip and herself.

LL: Wouldn't she have been quite vulnerable to an

exploration by the prosecution of the letters between herself and Philip?

DB: I suppose so. But Eqbal thought that she could speak of the letters with a charm and assurance and a sense of outraged privacy that would also be very moving, very persuasive.

So he made that pitch. And there was a strong negative response, especially on the part of Philip. He stated flatly that, first of all, the relationship between himself and Elizabeth was such that he could never allow her to undertake this risk unless he did so also. That, in effect, if she were alone upon the stand, she would be asked to assume the whole burden of the trial, and this was intolerable. From the human point of view, it left out the modifications, the feelings, the different lives and directions of the other people; it precluded any understanding on the part of the jury of the deep relationships involved; and it simply made her a kind of a "fall gal" for the whole show. Phil's feeling was that either everyone would take the stand or no one, that any compromise would be unfaithful to all involved.

LL: Where did Liz stand on the question of who should testify?

DB: As I recall, Liz took a minimum part in the discussion that night. But she had talked with everyone for many days before. I think our common understanding was that she was willing to take the stand if the majority should vote to have a limited defense.

LL: Was this discussion about who should testify influenced by a directive from the lawyers?

DB: There were lawyer-defendants meetings almost every day after the court proceedings, in the federal building. I had been present at one such meeting that

) 174 (

same afternoon, before we went to the jail to see Phil again. And there seemed to be a clear understanding that whatever decision was taken by the defendants would be respected by the lawyers. Given those lawyers it was predictable that they would feel this way.

On the other hand, I had talked individually the night before with Ramsey Clark. His strong feeling was that nothing was to be gained by going on with a defense, that whatever followed would be a vicious manhunt, especially against Philip. The narrow rules of the court and the subjection of the judge to the worst initiatives of the prosecution had made two things inevitable: 1) denial of motions for immunity for defense witnesses; and 2) exclusion from the court of any political issues in the course of the defense. I wouldn't say Ramsey was discouraged that night; rather, I had a strong feeling he had come to a new sense of the reality of things and was simply sharing it with me; that he was saying: This is how I see it as an experienced lawyer, and this is my hope with regard to the decision of the defendants.

Anyway, getting back to the meeting that Wednesday night at the jail, I should have mentioned that defense lawyer Terry Lenzner was also present, by invitation of the defendants. His strongest contribution was to outline for the defendants the reasoning of the lawyers with regard to stopping the show at that point. That is, that politically the scene was barren; and from the point of view of legal jeopardy, a defense would offer the government a field day. It would offer a wider cast of the net against the Catholic Left of the East Coast, using certain of the defendants and maybe all of them, depending on who took the stand, as bait.

LL: In other words, the lawyers were in agreement in

recommending that there be no defense presentation, but they were asking the defendants to make up their own minds?

DB: I'm not even sure that they put it in the form of a recommendation. It was rather a weather report from the experts about the strictly legal risks of undertaking a defense in this atmosphere. The recommendation was obviously implicit, but they did not cast it in that form, quite deliberately, I think.

LL: Did you personally agree with Phil's position, or with that of the majority?

DB: Could I step back a little bit from the question? Again, I am caught in a complexity of feeling about my place in the trial and the validity of my voicing any opinion at all. I would say that my deepest feeling was one of respect for the decision taken by those whose heads were on the block.

Let me put it this way: I hope that if I had been a defendant I would have sided with Phil on the side of risk, of the necessity of taking the chances of a defense, simply because the link between the death of the Vietnamese and the trial had never really been closed and had to be closed in whatever way and at whatever risk.

However, my respect embraced the four who saw the trial differently from Philip and myself. I believe that the friendships that emerged from the trial—that trial by fire—will be something to offer the future. It's much more important that everyone who voted as a defendant came out with a sense that he was unviolated, undestroyed, than it would have been to come out as bearers of a superior politics which ignored human damage.

LL: The reports in the press about this dramatic decision by the defendants not to present a defense did not explain it very clearly. For example, I don't think most people yet understand the importance of the question of immunity for the witnesses whom the defendants would have called. Wasn't the judge's refusal to grant defense witnesses immunity also a motivating factor in their decision?

DB: Yes, it was. To me this is further evidence of the sensitivity toward others that was alive among the defendants. It was so important to them that nobody should be summoned to the stand as a witness on their behalf who thereby could become a subject of further prosecution or be forced to reveal the names of people involved in other draft board actions. And this was not merely a matter of demanding an immunity that had already been granted to the prosecution witnesses, but a simple postulate of human beings functioning together in a difficult time. That is, you couldn't summon people to help justify your life if it was going to cost them dearly in *their* lives. The only way, it seemed to me, of proceeding in a manner that would have been consonant with the humanism of the defendants, with their declared views of human life, would have been to guarantee immunity to defense witnesses. And that was not to be done, as the judge declared.

Meantime, many witnesses had been summoned to Harrisburg. I had one chance encounter with a couple of them that was special, striking, pathetic, sorrowful and amazing all at once, at least to my untutored ear and eye.

I went up to have lunch with Philip and found him not in the marshal's room, where we had always lunched together, but in the farther room, that adjoined the cage for prisoners in transit.

Anyway, there was Philip, resting against the bars,

talking into the cage where the two men were held, prisoners whom he had known in Lewisburg. One was a lifer with two forty-year sentences for kidnapping and manslaughter, and the other was beginning an eight-year sentence, as I recall, for embezzlement. They had never met me before, and they put two or three fingers out through the bars, and I put two or three fingers in, and we embraced in that idiotic enforced way and began talking, all of us understanding that we only had a few minutes because the marshals would discover us in this forbidden territory.

The two prisoners had consented to testify because, very simply, they loved Phil and they hated Douglas. They were willing to talk, amazingly enough, even if immunity were *not* granted. They were going to take their chances. And I knew, as did Phil, how rare this was— first of all that federal prisoners would even touch the situation of another prisoner while they were still behind bars; and secondly that they would do this when no immunity had yet been guaranteed, and indeed might not be.

Well, I think two things were clear: Douglas had committed the crime that criminals will not forgive: playing an informer's role while in prison. Also, their affection for Phil was such that it made them ready to embrace great risk that was not only rare but probably unique.

LL: Today is Good Friday. In Harrisburg, the jury has gone out and is deliberating. As you have said before, there have been many junctures between crucial events in your own life and the anniversaries of great symbolic importance in the Church. I wonder what feelings you are experiencing about that joining of ancient and contemporary themes as you meditate on Good

Friday and on the predicament of your brother and his friends in Harrisburg?

DB: I think somewhere in your question there lies a middle ground that might be fruitful for discussion. I have a sense, as well, of the danger at both extremes. That is, on the one hand, the symbol-ridden blindness of most churchmen who are content to go through the round of symbolic activity on these days without any "recognition scene" induced by the lives of people around them. And I think that's one special form of religious blindness that Jesus Himself had to confront in creating symbols that live, symbols that arise from human crisis, even from death. But at the other end of the spectrum there is something I would fear almost equally: to make pretentious ideological claims about Harrisburg that would see us too literally or obsessively as working out a passion play.

I think somewhere in the middle there are clues in the conduct of these Catholics that suggest a certain connection with the Passion story. Because they *are* believers, and because belief has led them into personal danger, into difficult decisions about their lives, into prison, and because they explicitly draw their resources from the gospel accounts of the trial and death of Jesus. This is beyond any doubt. Also, I think in these reflections the place of Boyd Douglas can be illumined, as long as one takes it easy. And I feel that I could gain some understanding of this man and his place in the trial, his place in the Passion account of the Seven, from a reading of St. Matthew's Gospel as well as from reading of the careers and tactics of other informers throughout history.

Perhaps Judas occupies a particularly malevolent and central position in the thinking of Christians. What strikes me most about these two turncoats is that each is a creature of the powers who are determined to destroy an interloper or troublemaker. No informer stands alone in history, exercising power over other lives independently of political or religious establishments. The informer makes no sense until he is connected with certain forms of authority that have made large claims on human conscience. In that sense he must be a creature, a second-string actor. He may initiate certain proposals to his own benefit, usually monetary benefit; but obviously he has put his life up for sale, for use by others, and is content to be used by puppeteers against good people who are making trouble.

LL: Then you don't regard Douglas * also as a person who, through some aberration of human psychology,

---

* Boyd F. Douglas, a fellow inmate with Philip Berrigan at Lewisburg Penitentiary, was the government's chief witness in the Harrisburg trial. Although serving three concurrent sentences for forgery and armed assault, he was the only Lewisburg prisoner permitted to attend the study-release program at Bucknell University, which allowed him to spend most of his time outside the prison walls. Douglas won Philip Berrigan's trust and began carrying letters between Berrigan and his supporters, copies of which he secretly turned over to the FBI. He also met personally with Berrigan's friends, posing as a committed revolutionary and encouraging them to engage in acts of violence and destruction, and kept the FBI informed of his conversations. The intercepted correspondence between Elizabeth McAlister and Philip Berrigan was the government's central "evidence" in its unsuccessful effort to prove the defendants had conspired to kidnap Henry Kissinger and destroy heating tunnels in Washington, D.C., Douglas' testimony at the trial was instrumental in gaining convictions of the two on the charge of having exchanged illicit letters, under the federal statute forbidding the passing of "contraband" in or out of federal prisons.

During his lengthy cross-examination at the Harrisburg trial, Douglas acknowledged a long history of criminal convictions for lying, embezzlement and impersonation (using as many as ten different aliases).

has become a pathological liar? Is he not also someone who lives in a fantasy world which, coincidentally, happens to come down on the defendants in a conspiracy trial in Harrisburg? He has a history of all kinds of fantasy activity; yet you seem to regard Douglas as being at the fulcrum of a whole context of political forces that are operating on him and forcing him to play a role.

DB: I think that after a time that was undoubtedly true. He went a certain way into a bargain with the government and, to that degree, step by step lost all personal initiative in this instance. That is not to say that he wasn't playing all sorts of interesting games, even with the FBI. But his freedom of activity, lying under the kinds of threats they laid down, made him, after a time, not much more than a puppet. He was forced to follow very closely the instructions of his masters, whether it was to wire himself for a conversation or to collect people for a party at which they would be under strict surveillance. Each step, under the threat of new charges, rendered him less and less a free agent.

Seeing Douglas in action brought me strongly back to the prison scene. The figure of Douglas, the immoral physiognomy of a man like that, is such a familiar sight, such a stereotype. I don't mean that there is a large number of talented informers in prison; I mean that, especially at a place like Danbury, the adage about "honor among thieves" doesn't hold very strongly. There's a great deal of dishonor among thieves. Which is not to deny that there is a great deal of dishonor among all kinds of criminals. But I lived in prison mostly among thieves. And Douglas was a thief. Violent crime in his life was either nonexistent or extremely incidental. But among people whose lives have been misshapen by attitudes towards money, a Douglas is an extremely familiar sight. He is always hanging around the FBI headquarters in spirit. That is to say, he's always available; whether he's in the courtroom or under questioning or in prison, he's for sale.

I also found that Hannah Arendt's characterization of Eichmann as banal was strikingly true of Douglas. There's a certain atmosphere around such men, their style, their way of talking, their way of coming on at people—that truculence and boldness and weakness in the gaze and the instinctive gestures. Born losers who have had to create a façade behind which they can come on tough and strong, with a certain machismo. It has sexual overtones, of course, because those people play women as they play the Market or the horses or the FBI. And after a certain long period in this sort of novitiate that Boyd Douglas underwent in the last year, the method became quite perfected. He could stand up under heavy grilling and a lot of heat and still, in that essentially immature way, could, as they say, come on strong. To put it negatively: he could not be cracked, nor could he be converted by the sight of his victims.

LL: Obviously you believe Douglas's testimony was a fabric of lies. Do you think he believed his story completely, that he was living the story he told? Or do you think that he is just a consummate liar who knew he was lying but had perfected his story to the point where he couldn't be cracked?

DB: I don't know how to answer that question. I think it's an extremely difficult one, and I doubt that many psychologists, even after long study of a man like that, could come up with a completely satisfactory theory. There are so many elements in his life that are more or less consciously at work in the decisions that he's making. He simply doesn't yield very easily to an analysis that would help others connect with him. I think it's at least possible that he has grown so used to lying and has had such inducements to lie and such long practice in the skill of lying that a kind of second life has become his real life. He would find it very hard to distinguish friend from enemy, good from evil, the moral summons issuing from the lives of the defendants from the summons of the FBI upon his conscience.

What is really fascinating is the large, almost exclusive place that money has come to play in his life over a long number of years. What he needed more than women or good clothes or freedom was money. And, as we know, he endangered his own health in submitting to medical experiments for money. Then along comes an opportunity to make it once and for all, evidently, and to have in one heap all these things that constitute the fantasy life of the crook. No wonder his life in a sense comes together around that tremendous beckoning in which every goody he's ever wanted is heaped in the bakery window, and he's got the key to the door.

Douglas also reminds me of the seventeenth-century English informer and provocateur, Topcliffe, who accomplished the ruin of many of the Jesuits in England. His way of getting at the priests was to play upon the most sensitive areas of their life, sacraments and ministry and preaching.

Topcliffe converted to Catholicism and followed the Jesuits about in their travels, in their efforts to minister to the Catholic minority. He had full access to them because he was knowledgeable about the countryside, knew the leading Catholic families and their whereabouts, and was able to offer a clever and well-wrought cover for their movements. All the while, of course, he was in close touch with the *poursuivants* of Elizabeth.

Topcliffe didn't hesitate to receive the sacrament, to have his sins forgiven, to enter into the most sacred areas of Catholic life and practice, in order to allay suspicion, to keep the priests dangling at the end of a noose and to help round them up when the moment arrived. He always wanted to be present, as the accounts tell, at the public executions, and actually was sprinkled with the blood of one of his victims.

LL: So you think there are some literal analogies to be drawn between the status of the Jesuits in Elizabethan England and that of the Catholic Left in this country?

DB: I think there are some interesting points in common, especially in the use of informers to bring people to heel. Of course, the increasing use of such people today is a cause of great concern. If government cases have to involve the degradation of human beings to this degree, then we're saying a great deal not merely about our treatment of the Vietnamese but about our treatment of one another. The meaning of Harrisburg is, to my judgment, not merely that an attempt has been made out of very flimsy material to destroy or utterly discredit seven people. It seems to me that the only damage worth speaking about has been done to Douglas, as well as to those who believe that psychological manipulation in the service of untruth could be of benefit to anyone.

I often think of Mr. Lynch, the prosecutor, and those FBI agents who described their relationship with Douglas over a year or more—the straight-faced, brazen, puritanical ethic that was revealed there. They were incapable of an embarrassment appropriate to what they had done. They felt no shame, and evidently they see no alterations in their lives or relationships as a result of such dirty work. I suppose one could carry one's wonderment much higher, because these decisions were made at the top level.

In the courtroom, though, one always had the feeling that Douglas was being put forward not merely as star witness but as fall guy. If anyone was going to endure the contempt of the decent public, that contempt should stop with *his* life and *his* activity. It should by no means fall on the higher authorities who had created him and destroyed him.

LL: The defendants often made it clear that their feeling toward Douglas was primarily compassion rather than hatred, because they regarded him as a troubled individual whose troubles were being exploited by the government.

DB: Compassion was certainly an element in my reaction to him, but that compassion would have been a little too easy if it had been the only thing I felt. I also felt anger, and I also felt it necessary to attribute responsibility to him. After all, he had known Phil over a period of time, had been exposed to some of the finest people one could ever hope to meet. He had been in a position of advantage, equal to that of any prisoner at Danbury or Lewisburg who was seeking some light on his life or some possibility of change. He had had that invitation open to him, not merely from Phil but from Phil's friends outside.

I'm suggesting that he too came to a crossroads; there he decided that he was going to play it crooked, was going to betray. I would feel a little easier about compassion toward him if he had never known Phil, or if he had only heard about Phil and then been urged to betray him. Or if he had only come to know Phil after he had chosen to work peace people over and to make money off them. If he hadn't had the exposure to all the defendants and to many others on the campus.

I think his choice, when he made it, was about as enlightened a choice as a human being can come to, given everything. Most people in prison never have the kind of exposure, the offers of help, the idealism, the powerful examples of moral goodness that Douglas had. So I think it would reduce our sense of the truth to look upon him merely as a puppet or a victim. There's more to it than that, more complexity, more responsibility.

LL: You seem to be operating on the assumption that Douglas was capable of reaching an enlightened decision, given the kind of alternatives that you suggest he was presented with. But isn't it also possible that Douglas is the kind of a person who might have been psychologically incapable of even understanding the choice that was offered to him, because he lives in a world of his own fantasies?

DB: I have great difficulty with that theory. In fact I couldn't verify it in him or in any prisoner I've ever met. It would be interesting if Phil could respond; he has been exposed to so many more different types of prisoners than I. I could never deal with a prisoner on the supposition that he is beyond redemption because of his background or fantasies or weakness. I think the only hope that we can hold out to men in prison who have long histories of bad trips and bad dealings is this: in friendship with someone who is strong and decent and concerned, change can occur. And I would begin with Charles Manson or with Sirhan Sirhan or with any one of the pariahs whom the public has condemned to hell. I suspect evidence that says a man cannot respond to the presence of moral goodness and the invitation it offers him.

LL: I was not suggesting that Douglas was beyond

redemption. But you seem to be saying flatly that, in the presence of goodness and community and love, any man, no matter how psychologically disturbed for however long, will recognize what is being offered him. And I question whether that is universally true.

DB: I could connect much more with what you're saying if it were applied to certain people in power rather than to powerless criminals. I had a more active despair about the conversion of Mr. Hoover than I have about any criminal I've ever met. Or about Mr. Lynch turning his life around than about Boyd Douglas doing the same. I don't mean to be hyperbolic or absurd; I'm trying to be as factual as I know how. I think that criminality is hardly ever present in convicted criminals. A much more difficult and practically untouched area of criminality lies in misused intelligence, the thirst for power, and the selling of one's life to a system that can, for example, prosecute the Harrisburg Seven with a clear conscience.

LL: It may very well be that there's a consonance between Douglas' predicament and the moral predicament of people like Lynch and Hoover and others in power. I just meant to suggest that it may be that Douglas found, at some stage in his life, that the only way he could survive in the world was to manipulate it; and that, having operated on that assumption over a long period of time, it would be terribly difficult for him to entertain the idea that another kind of life, a life where people gave to each other instead of taking from one another, where there was love instead of manipulation, was possible and open to him. But perhaps this is a tangential conversation.

DB: To me it's a very important subject; it goes to the heart of the matter. And I must say that Phil's statement toward the end of the trial, that he still wanted to be Boyd Douglas' friend, says everything I'm trying to say. That is, he hopes for the redemption of a man whom society has branded as beyond hope. What society is saying to Douglas is: "We won't take back our money; go off and hang yourself." It's the Sanhedrin talking to Judas. And this is a tactic that one must refuse if he's going to share in the ethic of the New Testament.

I have had enough experience in and out of jail to distrust psychiatry almost as much as I distrust religion. I feel that about the only thing we have going for us in the direction of change or rebirth or conversion is the presence, friendship, patience, and the long-term challenge offered people like Douglas by people like Philip and our friends, and myself too. Let me be arrogant for a moment. We knew that the only thing that happened in Danbury worth talking about happened because of us. There were shrinks and chaplains and educationists and guards all over the place; they came pouring in day after day. And nothing happened, literally nothing.

Maybe in trying to understand Boyd Douglas we're really coming to a little better understanding of the corruption of those professions which are in the service not of rehabilitation but of "law-and-order." I do believe that a real window opened for Boyd Douglas, and that he decided to shut it again. I can't prove it, but maybe I can convey to you some of my complex feeling that he needs to be confronted with what he did to Philip and the others. I don't mean legally speaking; I mean in the arena of conscience. And I say this, believe it or not, not as a way of putting him down but of asserting his dignity, because I still hold him to be a human being. If I decided that he was beyond the judgment of his own conscience or the judgment of God, I would be agreeing with the attitude of those who have used him and now want to throw him into the gutter.

LL: Without the agency of Boyd Douglas in the prison as intermediary between Philip and Elizabeth and his contacts with their friends, there would have been no indictment, obviously. Why do you think Philip trusted Douglas so completely that he gave such important letters to him and encouraged Sister Elizabeth to do the same?

DB: He trusted Douglas because he trusts everybody. That's the way he comes on in life. That also explains how he exerts such large moral power around him, why he's such an attractive or repulsive force, depending upon the way one views him. As far as I know, he did a prudent check on Douglas with those who should have known him. Evidently, part of Douglas' genius was the ability to conceal a great deal of his life and activities from the crop of prisoners he was living with. As Phil said, old cons who could smell a rat a mile away told him that Douglas was absolutely trustworthy. And it was on their word that he went to Douglas with these letters.

Of course, what was a source of great anguish to Phil was not so much that his trust had been betrayed as that the liberal community, especially the liberal media, were so ready to say that he'd been naïve or childish in putting these things down on paper and entrusting them to Douglas. And I think that, for a strong man, the derision and covert mockery of weaklings is the hardest thing of all to bear. He felt that such critics had themselves done nothing in a very bad time, that most of them were parasitic newshounds with their noses itching for big headlines, big ego, or big violence rather than standing for something in a violent time. Therefore they, along with the public they served, had very little right to judge him, since the only harm he had ultimately done was to people who were in the same moral position as himself and who had the same strength to respond to it and were ready for what came down.

The media were really playing the government game by characterizing him as a naïve fool. And by expecting that he should feel deeply ashamed of himself for being a fool, that he should even make some sort of public declaration of how foolish he had been, as a way of winning the forgiveness of the media freaks. Meanwhile, he felt that no matter how badly things had turned out, he and his friends were exonerated because they had done something that was in a tradition. They had tried something to stop the bloodletting.

This is a side of Phil that he had no opportunity of making evident at the time. So it is good to speak of it here. He said he would never change his attitude toward prisoners or resisters or his friends as a result of what had happened. Especially, he would go on living as if people were trustworthy, because to do anything else would be to join the mass of people who in one way or another are breaking communities apart instead of forming them. So he would continue to take his chances; though I have no doubt that both of us were more careful about letters and confidences after this thing occurred.

LL: I suppose that if you're in a movement which involves covert planning and activity and discussion, you can't trust everybody uniformly.

DB: Well, at the time when Phil was dealing with Douglas he was not trusting everybody. He didn't hand his letters around to be read by seventeen hundred prisoners. He trusted one man with a very dangerous kind of secret activity and was betrayed by him. And I think the betrayal had shattering personal consequences to Philip. But what I'm trying to suggest is that the experience didn't make him suddenly turn bitter or disillusioned about people. He still came on as a candid, open-hearted, friendly person.

The point is, he was never stupid about things. He tried for one alliance based on what he thought was a genuine friendship, and it failed. And I think the mark of his greatness is that a profound betrayal did not turn him into a less valuable Christian or a less valuable advocate of prisoners. And it won't, no matter what the outcome.

LL: It has often been suggested, I think with good reason, that the government's main purpose in bringing these people to trial was that of discrediting the Berrigans and what is called the Catholic Left. So that gaining a conviction on evidence, while it might have been of some value, was really a secondary priority. I am thinking particularly of the fact that the government attached Xerox copies of two of the evidentiary letters to the indictment at the time it was released, nine months before the trial started. And then, of course, we know that the government had tried even earlier to leak other letters to various newspapers and magazines. To many of us, this seemed much more like a smear effort than an attempt to hold a fair trial.

DB: I think most people tend to become traumatized at the extent of the official perfidy surrounding this trial. A like perfidy surrounds many efforts, both legal and legislative, to get the country into a law-and-order box —the theory being that the box has been opened and all sorts of evils are loose, including Catholics who have either gone crazy or gone criminal.

) 191 (

But I guess what I'm trying to understand is what real knowledge might be these days, when everybody has access to facts that can either drive him crazy or paralyze him morally or otherwise destroy him. I think Philip and the other defendants have suffered very little of this traumatic reaction. I don't think I've suffered much of it either. Of course I wasn't in this trial, but I've been through jail and underground. What I'm trying to express is that there must be a way of knowing the facts of life and of trying to deal with them.

There must have been some parallel in Germany in the thirties; one would have recognized that filthy waters were rising around him and that he must stem the deluge somehow. Or at the time of Stalin, it must have become clear over a period of time that irreversible, iron events were destroying people, that they were generally helpless, that perhaps there was nothing to be done except to stand somewhere, you know?

At this point in my experience I'm reduced to thinking with Bonhoeffer that maybe all we can do is to *stand somewhere* in the years to come. That the idea of "turning things around" is becoming a more and more empty, debased, useless political promise drawn from the rhetoric of the early sixties.

LL: "Engineering change"?

DB: Something like that. All one can do is know these things, admit the truth, the facts of life before one, and yet remain morally supple and available to people, even if one's effort isn't going to accomplish a great deal. In contrast, I think the history of the sixties up to this day is one of the absorption of facts as a destructive factor in one's development. It's as though one were condemned to eating shredded newsprint every day and became so ill he died of it, simply disappeared from the scene. So much bad news is about that one becomes incapable of creating any good news out of his own life.

To me, this is one way of putting the true criminality of Philip and the others: this has not happened to them. The worst government efforts have still not been able to turn them into papier-mâché corpses or the kind of frightened clerics that one sees all around these days, who are simply not able to cope with what is happening.

I can't imagine, for example, what it must be to believe in 1972 that it's still a project worthy of one's best energies to put out the editorial page of *The New York Times* every day. Yet I'm sure that's looked upon in certain circles as a rather prestigious project. I guess I'm interested in the distinction that Cardinal Newman drew in the nineteenth century between real knowledge and notional knowledge. Notional knowledge is the assimilation of facts leading nowhere; whereas real knowledge is some mysterious alchemy whereby the truth of existence, including the facts, leads one to moral development or simple action on behalf of people, on behalf of actual needs. At least that distinction throws some light upon the difference between the media people, whether they are creating, transmitting, or absorbing the news, on the one hand; and on the other hand, people like the defendants at Harrisburg, who have doggedly stuck to a few very simple and basic truths and followed through on them. Perhaps they have been clumsy, inarticulate, childish, self-contradictory—anything that sophisticated people want to throw at them, let them throw. I'm trying to understand the essential standing free and firm that they have been capable of. I think such virtue, in any long run that remains to us, is going to be crucial. And let the world make of it what it will. That's always been a good radical Christian cry, whether Lutheran or Catholic: we stand somewhere.

LL: It seems to me that Newman's distinction between notional knowledge and real knowledge, as applied to the American mass media, is entirely relevant. In general, most of the "knowledge" transmitted daily to the American public by newspapers and TV news is "notional knowledge"—fact devoid of context, analysis and interpretation. Part of the reason is editorial, part is economic, part is the laziness of many reporters, and part is the "cult of objectivity" with which American journalism has been infected for decades. But whatever their shortcomings, the media are almost the only means available for communicating with public opinion in this country. You are forced to deal with them and play their games—you have no choice. And in light of the superficial way in which the press "covered" both your underground experience and the Harrisburg trial, don't you feel at times the task is hopeless?

DB: Phil and I used to talk often at Danbury about Gandhi's unkillable optimism about the goodness of people. Gandhi used to say, "If we can present the truth, people will respond." And of course the American instance is very difficult to stay with because the media are not the people; the media are between you and the people; and, as you've already said, so much gets screened out in this process, denatured and watered down. But I think an element of understanding social change and our place in it is this kind of optimism—that you simply don't give up on the people. And that means that you don't give up on the media either. I must say I agree with that, for all my traumas, my nausea, my consciousness of how they twist and bend the truth.

It occurs to me also that we have almost no instance in the history of the West where the relationship between word and action, between the intellect and the activist, has been consistently and publicly available. I was struck recently by an interview with Sartre in *The New York Times*, in which he said that at this stage in his life he was finally realizing that he belonged in the streets. I think it came about because the students gave him that lead in 1968, when the upheaval took place in Paris. And now, in times of crisis, he believes he must be heard from, he takes his intellect into the streets, he distributes handbills, joins in picket lines and strikes. I connect his remarks with a book I read earlier called *The Betrayal of the Intellectuals*, which traced through the history of French culture the invariable betrayal, in times of social crisis, of the people by the intellectuals. Not that they went over to the other side; but they were silent, they were unheard from.

The religious analogies to this are very striking. The liberal credo would be to the effect that the word has a saving impact on people. I don't know where that's drawn from. It's certainly not Christianity, except in a debased, hardly recognizable way. The Christian creed states that the Word made flesh saves, a very different thing entirely. "In the beginning was the Word," but the Word did not become a saving principle until it was made flesh, until the enfleshment of the Word allowed the Word to be subject to human malice and contracted by liars and invaded by an informer and judged by the powers of synagogue and state, and therefore finally subject to death. Until the truth had undergone this tremendous inhuman testing and defeat, nothing happened for human beings.

To get back to where we started, I think that that has something to say about the absurd hopes of the man who puts out the editorial page of *The New York Times*.

It seems to me that until his life is somewhere, everyone from Rockefeller to Nixon will read his mild strictures upon their activity day after day and still send the bombers or gunmen out.

8

LEE LOCKWOOD: Obviously, your opposition to the war
hasn't altered since you went to jail. But has your analysis of how the war should be resisted changed as a result of your eighteen months in prison and the events
that have occurred since you went to prison?

DANIEL BERRIGAN: I could say something bathetic,
something that everybody realizes more and more every
day: that any significant public form of resistance is
going to meet with the harshest kind of "legal" reprisal.
And that's a terrifying deterrant to good people. But
it's one of the facts of life today. The very fact of certain
people coming together to discuss questions of their society is going to involve more and more jeopardy, more
and more threat of conspiracy charges.

While I was in jail I read the magnificent memoir by the wife of the Soviet poet Mandelstam, *Hope Against Hope*. It gives one icicles along the spine to ponder her appraisal of the growth of terrorism in the late twenties and early thirties, when Stalin came to power. People progressively forgot how to be themselves as the atmosphere of terror crept into the common life; they developed shells like crawfish or underwater creatures merely in order to survive. They simply forgot how to be normal and open in communication with others, how to expect decency and trust as the ordinary responses of people.

I don't want to be theatrical about it. But I think that legal moves like the Harrisburg indictments upped the ante on even the most basic human responses to human beings, made it much more difficult for ordinarily good people to grow in goodness. Which I take to be one way of putting our common task.

A man would be a fool to try to predict the other end of events. Let me say this: for anyone who wants to lay something on the line there's going to be considerable suffering and dislocation. Either of two things will happen: either resistance will become the commonly accepted norm of life for larger numbers of people, or they will recoil in fear, and people like ourselves will be progressively isolated simply because no one wants to be around lepers. I don't know which will happen.

While I was in prison I often thought, for instance, of my own family, especially my mother. She is eighty-six, and it's a terrible thing to know that your actions are bringing such suffering to an older person. On the other hand, one tries to balance this off with other factors; for example, in Vietnam, for an older person to suffer would be taken for granted as a "wartime occurrence." To compare that kind of suffering with the American peace movement is one way of saying that we are unused to any kind of suffering at all. Underdeveloped in the truest sense, that of spirit.

LL: In considering why the peace movement has failed to end the war, do you think one reason is that it has never developed an ample analysis of what is wrong with American society?

DB: No. I believe that the analyses have been coming in at a great rate. The evidence has been in for a long time, in some detail and with scientific rigor, that things are wrong. But I think these analyses proceed most often from the wrong academics. We have not yet been able to develop a revolutionary scholarship that would give new perspective to the evidence by joining it to the necessity of historical action. Except for people like Zinn and Chomsky and a few others, that has been extremely rare. The academics themselves are part of the game. Even in amassing evidence *against* the game, they continue to play.

At the same time, I want to underscore my conviction that a great deal of patience is required. The near future, like the present, will be marked by periods of intensity and periods of slackness. We cannot write a timetable ahead of time; we simply cannot know in advance what is going to work and what is going to peter out. We're too close to the beginnings; we're too close to trial-and-error yet. We just don't have the amassing of experience and time that would justify conclusions.

LL: Are you speaking now about thoroughgoing changes in American society in general or about the antiwar movement in particular?

DB: I'm speaking about both, because I stand with both very closely. I just don't think that the kind of power which has been mounted in Vietnam is going to be displaced as easily as we had hoped. Because the displacing of that kind of power is the shaking of the foundations of the society itself. It means the dismantling of the military as we know it; it means a new look at allocations of national resources, of wealth, brains and money; it means a new move in all directions. And the war is too close to the hearts and pocketbooks and planning of the technocrats for its ending to be seen as simply one easy project among others.

But I want to stress here the tragic import of ending the war. This is a first priority for decent people, and we're just beginning to encounter the great difficulty involved in achieving it. I think many people have looked at Vietnam as if it were, say, another adventure—the Marines slogging into Central America, another easy five-day joust. Easy in, easy out, and expendable lives inbetween. But we're finding out something tragically different, on both sides.

LL: You think that the antiwar movement assumed that it was going to be *easy* to end the war?

DB: At the beginning, we had vivid illusions about it. When it became apparent how difficult it would be, a chasm opened between the men and the boys, and there was a great peeling-off. Most of us had thought that ending the war could be an extracurricular matter, a matter of keeping everything we had, including our good name, our security clearances, our jobs, our homes, our incomes, of making minor adjustments which in no way would impugn our main moral direction or politics or foreign policy. And that illusion still persists!

LL: And is this illusion—that the war could be resisted while other business went on as usual—the main reason why the movement has failed to end the war, in your view?

DB: Well, simply put, I think there has never *been* a movement in any real sense. Getting rid of that illusion is part of our growing up too. Maybe that's a bit harsh; if so, others can modify it. In my own view, there never was a sustained agreement that the first issue was to change our style: to lose something, if anything was to be gained. By that I mean something serious: I mean something like jail; I mean something like death; I mean comparing the losses that peace people might have to endure against the losses that have been endured by those fighting the war. And that cost is a heavy one. I mean getting closer to the Third World experience of war and peace and of the social reconstitution of man. I think that that achievement is going to come last of all in the First and Second Worlds. Last of all to us because everything in our lives, in our national income and in our control over the Third World, has immunized us against the real facts of life; the first of which, it seems to me, is that any serious change in human life comes very dear.

LL: Since it hasn't happened through political action, is it your hope that this revolutionary change will come about as the result of some kind of religious revival or renaissance? Of some new evangelical movement, perhaps?

DB: Thank God for this commercial! (Laughing) I've been cuing you in for half an hour!

I always want to run for the hills when I hear that kind of talk about religion. But it does seem to me that faith in God, where joined to a very acute, compassionate human sense, is still a valid tradition and can make its own small contribution. And after all, we can't speak of anything but small contributions these days, as far as I can see. So I'm peacefully contented this should be both small and a contribution.

But the Church at large and the Synagogue at large are just about as bad as the State at large and just about as abominable in action.

LL: Are resistance actions such as Catonsville still valid, or do you think that something new has to be found?

DB: I think that kind of action, in its generic meaning, is always going to be valuable. That is, the effort to point out the distinction between inhumanly misused property and the misuse of human lives through property. As long as our culture endures in its present course, it's going to be necessary to try to point out those distinctions. But decisions on specific tactics belong to the group involved.

LL: I want to go back to something you touched on in our television interview in August 1970, while you were underground. We were talking about violence in American society, and you said something I found both provocative and curious. You said: "I think that our society, in a base and inhuman sense, needs the Weathermen to be violent and even secretly hopes that they will be. That the society, just as it needs an army, and needs someone to kill, also needs someone to *be* killed, needs someone to hunt down—as it needs the Mafia, needs the Ku Klux Klan, and needs the Panthers."

I found that statement rich with perceptive overtones. It seemed to me that you were saying many things: that American society is violent; that the Weathermen and the Panthers are violent not only because they wish to be but also because America, in some profound way, *requires* them to be violent; and that one part of the movement, which ought to be providing a moral alternative to the society which it seeks to transform, instead both reflects and suffers from one of its essential sicknesses. To that extent, I suppose one might say: What is wrong with the movement is what's wrong with society.

DB: I have a simple-minded conviction that a movement, especially in a society like ours, is going to be historically useful only insofar as it is sensitive to the question of violence. I said this in my letter to the Weathermen.* Such sensitivity includes the fact that one is willing to be very circumstantial about things. I also like George Jackson's statement in his prison letters that he is willing to be as nonviolent as he *can* be, and he's willing also to be as violent as he *must* be. In the right hands, a principle like that is quite useful. In the wrong hands, it can be disastrous, of course; it depends on where one's life is and where it is going. But that formulation is very close to my own sense of things: not setting up a rigid norm drawn out of other cultures or other times, but trying to move as believing men and women in our own society—drawing upon other traditions available, from Jesus to Gandhi and Martin Luther King.

This need for violence we spoke of earlier necessarily invades the legal system and the courts. As the war goes on, and as the moral and intellectual justification for it becomes shabbier, certain people must be screwed to the wall in order to show the rest of society that this sort of dissent is not going to be tolerated. Political judgments about the lives and deaths of others are in the hands of a powerful clique and are going to be retained there. That state of affairs is going to have

* See appendix

to be maintained as long as the war is a politically hot issue, as it obviously still is.

So where does that leave us? It leaves us with a society the outreaches of whose violence invade even the legitimate structures of that society, in the name of illegitimate conduct in the world at large. This is very hard to speak of—it's very hard to face. It means that the recourse of decent men is constantly narrowing rather than widening, that their opportunities for a legitimate hearing through due legal process are constantly being eroded by the corruption of the process itself.

There's no doubt in my mind—there's no doubt in the minds of *any* thinking men—about the government's intention. In Harrisburg as in the trials of Ellsberg and Angela, the indictment *is* the conviction. The indictment is the justification of the society's national and international conduct. And, in that narrowing world where real justice is possible, good people are going to be squeezed harder and harder.

That is to say, violence is constantly putting on the gown, the wig and the soutane that legitimate it, whether in the university, in the courts or in the churches. Violence speaks with the voice of God, with the voice of justice, with the voice of intellectual enlightenment. In such a way, since war by its nature is total today, every structure must be totalized into the main enterprise. So the courts become another instrument of the war itself.

To the deepening reliance within our society upon violence as a means of resolving our problems, I tried to offer an alternative in my letter to the Weathermen. I was suggesting to the Weathermen that the course that they were on was not productive for the deeper meanings of the movement, for meeting the deeper needs of resistance today, and that we were trying to make possible another emphasis. I tried to stress the desperate ongoing need for communities that would endure, that could act with inner coherence and with a sense of responsibility toward one another, a sense of mutual dignity, of mutual forgiveness. I urged them to build communities based upon resources of the spirit and of the heart such as could offer some alternative to the public that was arrayed against them, that was trying to portray them as monsters, as innately violent people. I wanted to help destroy the mythology that was being created about the Weathermen.

LL: Was it only a myth being created *about* them? Don't you think they contributed to its creation?

DB: I would suggest that at the time they certainly were contributing to it, and that's what I was trying to have them take a look at, too: the fact that this wasn't a total pipe dream on the part of the society.

Well, it took months before anything happened, and it was not easy to wait that out. But I think it was probably worth the effort. In fact, the response was almost beyond my hope, because it indicated that they really were serious and were growing more thoughtful about such things. So it was very gratifying to have that news in prison, after all those months, that they had taken me seriously. That letter had been a shot in the dark, something like stuffing a message into a bottle during a shipwreck and tossing it overboard, hoping it would get to the right shore.

LL: We were talking about violence, and I would like to come back to that essential question about our society and the possibility of change. It seems ironic to me that it was the accusation of violence that underlay

) 205 (

the Harrisburg indictment, while it is also the accusation of violence that underlies your entire stand against the official forces of society.

DB: Right.

LL: Perhaps there is no simple answer to this question. But, if violence is so fundamental to our way of life, to our tradition, to our culture, if it infects our thought patterns and our automatic responses, if it is so uncontrollable—if it is "as American as cherry pie," as Rap Brown once said—where is the hope of redemption in all of this? Isn't it overly idealistic to believe that something so essential to our character can be changed?

DB: I can be hopeful because I'm modest even in my hope. I'm not carried away by messianism, by crusading, or by delusions about changing the world or the society. One begins with the hope that his life will be a sign of something for others, a sign which might be attractive, which might radiate a certain kind of human feeling, a sense of others. And if this is a minoritarian project, then so much the better! It's bound to be modest, especially in times like this. I can't conceive of God turning the society around, so *I'm* not about to break my back trying.

I would like to try to help reduce the quotient of needless and thoughtless suffering and of needless and thoughtless cruelty, to keep human beings open to the idea that it is possible to turn around. We can act in other ways than those officially sanctioned by a paramilitarized society. And if that sort of thing affects one person out of a hundred, or one out of a thousand, all to the good. I'm not interested in a body count. I'm interested in living as I perceive I am called on to live, and seeing whether or not that may be useful and attractive to others. And I am convinced it is, because I am convinced that we are setting the stage for things that are to come, if anything is to come. We are calling out to something inherent in the best instincts, the best soul, the best part of ourselves: a call to *be* human.

But, obviously, one is cut down to size in times like these, and he has to take that humiliation seriously, a bread which he breaks and eats every day, with the possibility that this may be his portion for the rest of his life. But I wouldn't want to leave it at that, because I think that to take *that* seriously is only another way of saying that one must take life seriously. And, because the inherent modesty of life is not taken seriously, the military metaphor rules: that of abstract death and abstract life, of abstract army commands issuing from distant authority, of abstract human beings.

LL: Are you saying that you're not interested in leading a movement or constructing an ideology or indeed in anything formal; that you are only interested in providing an example by your own actions that others might emulate, and that political change will ultimately take care of itself?

DB: I don't want to seem irresponsible or spineless. But the idea of leadership, and of all those quiddities connected with seeking first place over others, I can't buy. What is really of interest in the long run is people who ponder a certain consistent course of action, invite others to share their reasons for doing so, and then, as far as their own lives are concerned, let the chips fall where they may. People who act and then stand where they acted: those are the moral people as far as I can understand them. Everything else tends to rot or sour or fall away from its first purpose. I don't think that our work has, and I don't think it's about to.

LL: Perhaps it's premature to ask you this, but do you

) 207 (

feel that the ideas and issues that you were involved in when you went to jail are still alive and viable now, and that you still have a role to play?

DB: Well, I sense there are really two questions there. One of them is, Do I feel I can make a contribution? And, of course, I do, and want to very much. As to the other question about conditions in general, particularly the war, I feel very badly about that, obviously—coming out of jail and finding, with almost two years of my life gone, that so little has changed for the better and so much has changed for the worse, and that this irreversible course seems to be rolling ahead.

But I'm very consoled by the numbers of young Danbury ex-felons who went from prison to Harrisburg to help during the trial. I think that's a remarkable continuity. I guess I'm getting a sense that whatever is happening of any worth or human attractiveness is taking place around events like those: the trial, or my release. People take a certain breath of exhilaration from such things and go on from there. But I have an awful sense of the episodic character of things, the terrible distractions that rule people's lives these days.

Nobody seriously talks much about a "movement" any more. It seems to be one of those words that went out with the sixties. In that sense, Nixon has been brilliant; Nixon is a winner. Most people find that they can adjust their conscience and their life-style to the continuation of the war. The nation is big enough, there's enough space, there's enough professionalism, there's enough money to spell out a future that people will consent to. And that's horrible, of course. It means an amazing adjustment to a bloody situation. And Nixon has done it; he's made it. He has made the war extremely remote and abstract. He has washed the blood off his own page as far as the public goes. It seems as though the winy and rosy days of the early sixties were absolutely ephemeral; they're gone, and now you start all over again every day, I guess.

LL: Do you think the peace movement may have put too much emphasis on the war as the major issue, while the circumstances which produced the war and which permit the acceptance of violence by this society were not examined or articulated enough?

DB: Yes, I think one can say that, but I don't find it very helpful even after it's admitted. The real difficulty for young Americans is that technology has created a promised land for them and a horror elsewhere. The horrors of bad politics and bad technology are almost invariably felt elsewhere, except for the domestic poor and the blacks. But I'm talking about the middle-class movement. Our expectations of change were childish and moody; they were expressed in debased metaphors drawn from machines, from the power we think we have over things. In consequence, we think that we can engineer change of spirit. And when it doesn't happen—as God knows it hasn't happened—people fade, people fade. And young Americans are able to fade out with a very good conscience by the thousands. Of course the drug culture and their parents' arms are always awaiting them. The prodigal sons and daughters hitchhike home in droves. So it's hard to keep main issues main.

LL: But do you think the main issues have really been gotten at in the first place?

DB: Anybody who cannot appreciate that the war itself is a main issue is a stranger to my mind. Obviously, a sense of what the war is and where it comes from would lead one into a critique of the whole society. A strong sense of the wrongness of the war is one sign that a person has connected with the whole mix.

LL: Do you have a clearer idea of what is ailing American society as a result of your time in prison?

DB: A prison certainly gives one a view of the punishment that has habitually been wreaked upon those who are written off, those who don't make it. Prison offers the difference between realizing this in a remote sort of way and realizing it up-close, somewhat like a Vietnamese, a victim. But I don't want to overdo that, because I was in one of the milder prisons. I know quite well that I would not have survived in a place like Attica. I wouldn't have made it.

LL: Why not?

DB: I would die. I can't take that kind of life. I had enough trouble taking it at Danbury, God knows. But the idea of strict lockup and hatred and hostility and violence up-close—that would be too much, and I know it. It wouldn't be too much for Phil, but it would be for me.

Anyhow, to answer your question, I'm trying to recover a kind of rational time sense. It is quite dislocating to find that as one has changed in solitude, others in much more favorable circumstances have not changed. I'm speaking particularly of my fellow Jesuits, most of whom I find are just as comfortable and just as remote from an understanding of the suffering being wrought by the war as when I went to jail eighteen months ago. As far as the Jesuits are concerned, I might have been away for a weekend in Cuernavaca, for all they've changed.

This hits very hard. But on the other hand, I didn't come out of jail with that hope either, so the shock of what is not happening in the Church is mitigated. If I had been in the tiger cages in Vietnam for fifteen years and come back, I'm quite sure that the American Jesuits would be pretty much in the same stasis. And I'm pretty sure that I could take that too.

I guess that if you push hard and ask, "Well, then, what the hell are you hoping, or what does hope mean to you?" I would say that it's important for some of us to hang around and be visible in a way that stands true to the facts of life and the facts of death, and beyond that to be quite indifferent about things. I don't mean that as an inhuman statement, I mean it as a kind of Zen statement. To let all else flow, because anything else is interference, a mirror game with those who are engineering others to death.

I think you'll understand that to me this "hanging around" is a laconic way of putting something I regard as quite serious. It includes the effort to be as persuasive as one knows how about *why* one is hanging around, and inviting others to do the same. But I'm trying to set myself apart from any imposed necessity of winning the peace, as others are freneticized into winning the war. I don't believe that Christians are called to win anything. I think they're called to be in the right place at the right time for others, and then let Chicken Little do his damnedest. The cruelest thing that I have to face is not the fact that the Jesuits haven't changed; the cruelest thing for me, and I'm sure for Phil, is that the Harrisburg trial did not fulfill our hopes about what might be accomplished there, and how we might communicate through it. The trial, I am sure he feels, as I do, was a dud. It was a dud marked with blood and sweat. And that must be faced. That's much harder than the Church situation for me, and I'm sure for him.

LL: Is it part of your faith that the Kingdom of God is possible in this world? Do you believe that man is meliorable; that if people like yourself "hang around" long enough, bear witness strongly and courageously enough, eventually enough others will follow your example that the world will be changed according to the Biblical promise?

DB: First we might remind ourselves, at this hour of Good Friday in 1972, that we're commemorating an event in the course of which the Kingdom of God was reduced to one dead man and a few scattered friends, most of whom walked out on their friend's defeat as incomprehensible and intolerable. That says something, I think, to the question. Also, I think it's necessary to analyze the Biblical promise about everything turning out all right. It's certainly not offered in the sense in which the prosecutor at our trial at Catonsville said it about America. You remember those famous, vacuous words of Mr. Scolnick: "We are *going* to get better! Things *will* improve! But they will not improve, et cetera, et cetera, if the law is broken!" Well.

In other words, the Biblical statement is not a statement about cultures or about America at all. It's a statement about a mysterious intervention of God, who, in His own hour and time, a time hidden from all of us, steps in to set right that which was death-ridden and malicious and destructive. So the hope of Christians, and I am sure also of Jews, is not in any more-or-less miraculous conjunction of goodness and talent and technology as the sum of what man can build in history. The word of the Bible is shown in the lives of the prophets and especially the life of Jesus and in what He promises for the future. When man is most triumphant and powerful, things are invariably worse for the majority of people. And conversely, when the believers, or let's say even the remnant, are enslaved or exiled or in a desert circumstance, His intervention and His setting aright may be expected. Because this humiliation, this dearth of justice and peace and decency, arise before Him as a great cry for His intervention.

So the idea that things will get better if men are ethically good is a distinctly pagan acculturation of the Biblical promise. What God promises is that when things are at their worst it is still possible to believe, and that may be all God's gift for a long time, for a lifetime, for generations. That there is a community that itself intervenes by calling on Him.

In this sense, Harrisburg may be the intervention which makes it possible for God still to act, since man has presumed to seize almost everything in human life and claim it for death. As to the final shape of things, the Bible never dwells in complacence on man's achievement. The evidence seems to turn much in the other direction, that men will make such a mess of life that the only possibility is God's help; God must intervene. The apocalyptic literature is fraught with a terrible symbolism: world discord, famine, the death of multitudes, the defection of believers. It's only at this point that a righting of things can be hoped for.

I think that divine intervention, Biblically understood, does not mean that the power of God confronts human power. Such a statement draws its analogies about divine power out of human power, and then you're back in the same old game, instead of reading the Bible. It's much more according to the truth of things to say that, when God intervenes, He intervenes in the form of powerlessness confronting power. Now we could rightly speak of the powerlessness of believers as a new form of power. That's true as long as we understand that faith refuses to play the game of power in order to confront it. I want to be very concrete about this—a stubborn insistence upon the power of nonviolence confounds human power, and it's the only force that can do so. Because for every gun in our hand, there are several guns in the adversaries'. But when a man or woman says, "I have no guns—shoot me or respect my claims," then we have real intervention, as far as I'm concerned.

Again, I think that this is one way of putting the impasse, the perplexity, the fury of the government at Harrisburg. Mr. Lynch didn't know how to function with such people. He could only blow his stack twenty times a day, heap reproaches upon them, and seek to discredit them. I believe in sum that the moral stance, the courage and the radiance of those people *was* an intervention, the only kind I know of. It's so clear, in fact, that the Church is blinded by it. The Church cannot recognize it except in a very, very low-key way, here and there.

LL: It seems to me that the kind of "intervention" you're speaking of might be rather unsatisfactory, let's say, for a powerless Vietnamese peasant who has just lost his family under American bombs, or for any one of several million Indians or Pakistanis who have undergone equal suffering. I can't place people like that, who exist in this world literally by the hundreds of millions, within the context of the kind of intervention that you're holding out for.

DB: Well, I'm not sure that I was including them directly in what I was saying. I was talking about Christians who are in deep trouble with the law of the land in our country. Now, I guess what reaches across our situation into the troubles of the poor of the world is my conviction that guns will not bring change to Indians any more than they will bring it to Americans. And Harrisburg is offering this clue, which in another culture was also offered by Gandhi.

LL: I'm sure this question sounds rather dumb, and far too pragmatic for the understanding of a Divine Mystery, but—what does God do for these millions of powerless Indians and Vietnamese and even for those benighted Americans who are suffering their own kinds of hell? I mean, it seems very nice that a few people can be illuminated by the will of God, like those in Harrisburg, if that's what happened to them. But what does that mean for the possibility, whether present or ultimate, of justice and peace in the world for the billions of human beings who live in it?

DB: If I understand what happened at Harrisburg, it's one of the few things that is happening on behalf of those millions in the world. Certainly, in that trial, they hoped to articulate their connection with suffering everywhere, especially the suffering of the Vietnamese. I guess all I can do is to turn the question around and say, "What else is happening, what else is God doing on behalf of these people *except* raising up people like the Harrisburg defendants?" Unless one wants to have recourse to the next five-year plan of the State Department for the seeding of birth control pills over the Indian landscape or the seeding of bombs over North Vietnam.

I guess your question is one way of helping *me* understand more concretely the universal application of Harrisburg. From another point of view, I am a bit uncomfortable with the way in which you put the question, "What is God doing for these people?" I think that

Americans have an interesting way of disposing of God. As long as good things happen to people, they love to claim them for themselves. "We did it, keep God out of it." But when they bring something horrible down on people, they like to obscure their part in it and invoke God's silence or God's puzzlement or God's indifference. Our "religion" allows us to bomb the hell out of people and then complain, "Why didn't God intervene to save this situation?" While all the time, we are directly responsible for it.

LL: But haven't you been saying that if people like those in Harrisburg stand fast and firm and bear witness and embody the word of God, it will have resonance, it will have an effect eventually on power itself?

DB: No, I haven't. I wouldn't make that kind of claim at all. I think that that verges on an optimism that I can't deal with and that is not Biblical, as I understand the Bible. Concretely, the actions of the Catholic Left have meant a great deal to the country, as the country itself has disintegrated and as moral continuity has become rarer. People long for *something* in their midst that they can connect to, some stamina or courage. As things have gone, the Catholic Left are among the very few who have offered that. They have relieved to some degree the depressing reality of life—more bad news and less good people.

As for the future, I think a Christian is obliged to confess a great ignorance about it, even while he works and plans toward it. I don't think that he's allowed to indulge in the fantasies of five-year plans; at least I don't see any evidence that that's allowed. Strangely, this is the point at which I join the rightism of some churchmen who say that clerics don't belong in politics, clerics don't belong in the Congress. I say Amen to that. Of course they don't. Priests, ordained to the service of the Church, should stand in a critical relationship toward both Church and state.

LL: According to that reasoning, why is it any more appropriate for you to be in the Jesuit order than, say, for Father Drinan to be in Congress?

DB: I don't know really where to grab that. On the one hand, at least by supposition, the Jesuit order is supposed to be one organ of the good news of Jesus in the world. That's the hypothesis upon which I entered the order. The Society of Jesus is a way of being in the Church and of expressing one's faith there. Now, Drinan's being in the Congress is, let's say, a carousel horse of a different color.

LL: I think that's brushing off the implications of the question. Regardless of why you *entered* the Jesuit order, you stand in a very critical relationship to that order.

DB: "Critical" is the word! Right.

LL: Why then would it not be possible for a priest with the same set of assumptions as yours to be in Congress and to try to stand in critical relationship to its power?

DB: We're talking about such different things. In the Jesuit order I can still draw on the gospel through the lives of certain members, through certain communities and certain sacramental experiences. But for me to transfer the center of my understanding of the gospel to the Congress of the United States, speaking from that rostrum, having to be silent about the war, about prisoners, about the children of poverty; if I had continually to make these compromises because I am first of all an elected political animal and only secondly a minister of the gospel, then to my mind I would have disconnected

) 217 (

from the real tradition in order to accept a culturally bastardized pseudotradition. In effect, I would have denied the meaning of my ordination, which was to the Church for the promulgation of the gospel and for the spelling out of its ethical implications here and now.

LL: Well, maybe this is a dead-end avenue of conversation. But I think you would agree that there are some congressmen who have been extremely vocal, critical, and articulate of very minoritarian viewpoints, especially about the war. The fact that you are an elected official is not *necessarily* an inhibition against speaking your mind. It's only an inhibition if you become corrupted by the power you hold; when, say, the desire to be reelected becomes more important than saying the things that you would say out of your own spirit and heart.

DB: Here, we could get into a discussion which I think would be fruitless. What I would like to insist on is that our tradition does not allow the minister of the gospel to identify his life with the aims of public policy as a minister of that policy. This is true unless the Church is to be wedded to Caesar, unless throne and altar are to become one in aim and ethos and vision. If what you claim is possible, then the only workable arrangement is in Franco's Spain and in Constantine's Rome. And it seems to me that it is exactly these bloodstained periods that we're trying to undo, that we're trying to renounce, in order to gain some clarity and audibility about what the Church might be in a bad time.

Harrisburg: Holy Saturday, April 1, 1972
Address by Father Daniel Berrigan

I have a brief message to you who have come from far and near to share our agony over the fate of good men and women in a desperate time.

The tawdry, grotesque proceedings of the past months are over, and they have taught us a great deal: that human goodness is a mortally dangerous liability for Americans, even as human evil is a marketable asset. Philip Berrigan is in chains today; Boyd Douglas is a free citizen. That simple news must stick in your throat and mine, reading as we do this week the Passion story: "Then Judas, one of his friends, went to the chief priests and magistrates in secret and said, 'What will you give me and I will betray him?' And they appointed to him: 1500 dollars for capture of the Flower City people, 200 dollars for a letter leading to the capture of Daniel Berrigan, some thousands of dollars marked in their ledgers 'For services rendered.' Which is to say, he entered an agreement with them to deliver Jesus in secret."

When goodness is punished and evil rewarded, when the Son of Man goes to his death and the betrayer pockets his silver—when, moreover, Catholic FBI agents, Catholic prosecutors and Catholic informers savage the lives of nuns and priests—we may be sure that a new page has indeed turned in the history of our people and the history of the war.

Read with me the heading of that new page. It is entitled the twenty-fourth chapter of the gospel of Matthew. It says: "And Jesus was led from church to state, and condemned by both. . . . And informers came forward to condemn him, but their testimony did not agree; and Pilate washed his hands and said, 'I am innocent of the blood of this just man; look you to it' . . . And they crucified him there."

Which being translated to Harrisburg might read: "Domestic Vietnamization is complete. The pacification of peacemakers is successful. The war has come home." In the case of these troublemakers, in an older German phrase: "A definitive solution has been arrived at."

Dear friends, this is not a day to intoxicate ourselves with a rhetoric of power. If any of us were so retarded as to require still another lesson in the methods of war, Harrisburg would bring it home to us: *Before the overwhelming American assault on the rights and lives of innocent peoples, we Americans are as powerless and as expendable as the Vietnamese.*

Go tell that to your sons and daughters. Tell them Philip Berrigan has undergone nearly three years in prison for the crime of burning papers instead of children. Tell them the Harrisburg Seven thought of your children as they endured the Kangaroos and their court. Tell them the Passion story of Harrisburg, how perhaps it struck home to parents, teachers, priests who gathered here why this day is different from all other days. Tell your children that, in such times, prison may be honorable and freedom a disgrace. Share with them the bitter herbs which are the daily portion of those in exile, those in jail, those in courts, those in resistance, those in underground—those in graves.

And above all, and for Christ's sake, tell them that no man or woman was ever raised from the dead who had not first tasted death. How you came to understand this; how at Harrisburg you died a little, and got born a little. How you began to see, at least in measure, that the fury loosed on the Harrisburg Seven was rattling above you also. How, in Harrisburg, you began to grope along the narrowing passage into a human future; a choice, that is, between the conniving, guilt-ridden "good German" and the resisting criminal of peace.

Tell the children, please, that Philip and his friends and his brother embraced them at Harrisburg, and wished them well. Tell them we prayed that they might someday choose prison before killing, lives before property, official disgrace before bloodstained silver.

All of you, Jews and Gentiles, women and men and children, pass over with us, from death to life!

Appendix

On August 8, 1970, three days before his capture, Father Berrigan tape-recorded a message to the Weathermen which said, in part:

Dear Brothers and Sisters,

This is Dan Berrigan speaking. I want to say what a very deep sense of gratitude I have that the chance has come to speak to you across the underground. It's a great moment when I can rejoice in the fact that we can at last start setting up a dialogue . . . with a view to enlarging the circle of those who realize that the times demand not that we narrow our method of communication but that we actually enlarge it if anything new or anything better is going to emerge . . .

By and large the public is petrified of you.

There is a great mythology surrounding you—
much more than around me. You come through
in public as another embodiment of the public
nightmare which is menacing and sinister and
senseless and violent: a spin-off of the public
dread of Panthers and Vietcong, of Latins and
Africans, and the poor of our country, of all those
expendable and cluttering and clamorous lives
who have refused to lie down and die on command
or to perish at peace with their fate, or to exist
in the world as suppliants and slaves. . . .

The mythology of fear that surrounds you is
exactly what the society demands. . . . But it
also offers a very special opportunity to break this
myth that flourishes on silence and ignorance and
has you stereotyped as mindless, indifferent to
human life and death, determined to raise hell at
any hour or place. We have to deal with this as
we go along; but from where, from what sort of
mentalities, what views of one another and ourselves? Not from an opposite window of insanity
or useless rage, but with a new kind of anger
which is both useful in communicating and imaginative and slow-burning to fuel the long haul
which is the definition of our whole lives.

I'm trying to say that when people look about
them for lives to run with and when hopeless people look for hope, the gift we can offer others is so
simple a thing as hope. As they said about Che, as
they say about Jesus, some people, even to this
day, he gave us hope. So that my hope is that
you see your lives in somewhat this way, which is
to say I hope your lives are about something more
than sabotage. I'm certain they are. I hope the
sabotage question is tactical and peripheral. I
hope indeed that you are remaining uneasy about
its meaning and usefulness and that you realize

that the burning down of properties, whether Catonsville or Chase Manhattan or anywhere else, by no means guarantees a change of consciousness, the risk remaining always very great that sabotage will change people for the worse and harden them against further change. . . .

How shall we speak to our people, to the people everywhere? We must never refuse, in spite of their refusal of us, to call them our brothers. I must say to you as simply as I know how, if the people are not the main issue, there is simply no main issue and you and I are fooling ourselves also, and the American fear and dread of change has only transferred itself to a new setting.

This, I think, is where a sensible, humane movement operates on several levels at once if it is to get anywhere. So it is saying communication yes, organizing yes, community yes, sabotage yes—as a tool. That is the conviction that took us where we went. And it took us beyond, to this night. . . .

My hope is that affection and compassion and non-violence are now common resources once more and that we can proceed on that assumption, the assumption that the quality of life within our communities is exactly what we have to offer. . . .

No principle is worth the sacrifice of a single human being. . . .

When madness is the acceptable public state of mind, we're all in danger, for madness is not so much a phenomenon as an infection in the air. And I submit that we all breathe the infection and that the movement has at times been sickened by it too.

It has to do with the disposition of human conflict by forms of violence. In or out of the military, in or out of the movement, it seems to me that we had best call things by their name, and the name for this thing, it seems to me, is the death game, no matter where it appears. And as for myself, I would as soon be under the heel of former masters as under the heel of new ones. . . .

. . . I think our realization is that a movement has historic meaning only insofar as it puts its gains to the side dictated by human dignity and the protection of life, even of the lives most unworthy of such respect. A revolution is interesting insofar as it avoids like the plague the plague it promised to heal. Ultimately if we want to define the plague as death, and I think that's a good definition, the healing will neither put people to death nor fill the prisons nor inhibit freedoms nor brainwash nor torture its enemies nor be mendacious nor exploit anyone, whether women or children or blacks or the poor. It will have a certain respect for the power of the truth, which created the revolution in the first place. . . .

Instead of thinking of the underground as temporary or exotic or abnormal, perhaps we are being called upon to start thinking of its implication as an entirely self-sufficient, mobile, internal revival community, so that the underground may be the definition of our future. What does it mean literally to have nowhere to go in America or to be kicked out of America? It must mean to us: let us go somewhere in America, let us stay here and play here and love here and build here, and in this way join not only those who like us are recently kicked out also, but those who have never been inside at all, the blacks and the Indians and Puerto Ricans and Chicanos, whose consciousness has gone far under the rock.

Next, we are to strive to become such men and women as may, in a new world, be non-violent. If there's any definition of the new man, the man of the future, it seems to me that we do violence unwillingly, by exception, as instrument, knowing that destruction of property is only a means, and keeping the end as vivid and urgent and as alive to us as are the means so that the means are judged in every instance by their relation to the ends. I have a great fear of American violence, not only out there in the military and the diplomacy, in economics, in industry and advertising, but also in here, in me, up close, among us.

On the other hand, . . . I have very little fear, from firsthand experience, of the violence of the Vietcong or Panthers (I hesitate to use the word violence), for their acts come from the proximate threat of extinction, from being invariably put on the line of self-defense, but that's not true of us and our history. . . . We are unlike them, we have other demons to battle.

But the history of the movement, in the last years, it seems to me, shows how constantly and easily we are seduced by violence, not only as to method but as to end in itself. With very little politics, very little ethics, very little direction, and only a minimum moral sense, if any at all, it might lead one to conclude in despair: the movement is debased beyond recognition, I can't be a part of it. Far from giving birth to the new man, it has only proliferated the armed, bellicose, and inflated spirit of the army, the plantation, the corporation, the diplomat. . . .

The question now is what can we create. I feel at your side across the miles, and I hope that sometime, sometime in this mad world, in this mad time, it will be possible for us to sit down face to face, brother to brother, sister to sister, and find that our hopes and our sweat, and the hopes and sweat and death and tears and blood of our brothers throughout the world, have brought to birth that for which we began.

Thank you and shalom.

About the Author

DANIEL BERRIGAN, Jesuit priest, poet and nonviolent resister, has published a number of volumes of poetry;
Night Flight to Hanoi, a war diary; *No Bars to Manhood; Dark Night of the Resistance;* and other books.
He is also the author of the play *The Trial of the Catonsville Nine.*

LEE LOCKWOOD, author of *Castro's Cuba, Cuba's Fidel*, is a
journalist whose articles have appeared in leading magazines in the United States and abroad. He first met
Father Berrigan during Berrigan's "underground" days
when they collaborated on a documentary film called
The Holy Outlaw. They became friends, and Lockwood
was a regular visitor at Danbury.